Senior Executive Assessment

A Key to Responsible Corporate Governance

Dean Stamoulis

⟨W⟩WILEY-BLACKWELL

A John Wiley & Sons, Ltd., Publication

Blackwell Publishing was acquired by John Wiley & Sons in February 2007. Blackwell's publishing program has been merged with Wiley's global Scientific, Technical, and Medical business to form Wiley-Blackwell.

Registered Office
John Wiley & Sons Ltd, The Atrium, Southern Gate, Chichester, West Sussex, PO19 8SQ, United Kingdom

Editorial Offices
350 Main Street, Malden, MA 02148-5020, USA
9600 Garsington Road, Oxford, OX4 2DQ, UK
The Atrium, Southern Gate, Chichester, West Sussex, PO19 8SQ, UK

For details of our global editorial offices, for customer services, and for information about how to apply for permission to reuse the copyright material in this book please see our website at www.wiley.com/wiley-blackwell.

Library of Congress Cataloging-in-Publication Data

Stamoulis, Dean.
 Senior executive assessment : a key to responsible corporate governance / Dean Stamoulis.
  p. cm – (Talent managment essentials)
 Includes bibliogrpahical referneces and index.
 ISBN 978-1-4051-7958-4 (hbk. : alk. paper) – ISBN 978-1-4051-7957-7 (pbk. : alk. paper)
 1. Executives–Rating of. 2. Executives–Psychological testing. 3. Executive ability–
Evaluation. 4. Employment tests. 5. Emplyee selection. I. Title.
 HF5549.5.R3S686 2009
 658.4'07125–dc22
                                                                              2009005145

A catalogue record for this book is available from the British Library.

Icon in Case Scenario boxes © Kathy Konkle/istockphoto.com

Set in 10.5 on 12.5 pt Minion by SNP Best-set Typesetter Ltd., Hong Kong
Printed in Singapore by Ho Printing Singapore Pte Ltd

1   2009

To Ashley, Caroline, Thomas, and Jack, for your constant support and love. To my father Thomas, who taught me the importance of a keen eye and a curious mind, and who will always be my inspiration.

Contents

Contents

Series Editor's Preface ix
Preface xi
Acknowledgments xiii

Chapter 1 The Case for Senior Executive Assessment 1

Why CEOs and Boards Tend Not to Know a Lot about
    Senior Executive Assessment 2
Why CEOs and Boards Are Wary of Senior Executive
    Assessment 5
What Is Senior Executive Assessment? 6
The Benefits of Senior Executive Assessment 8
New Expectations about Corporate Governance 10
Summary 13

Chapter 2 Purposes 15

A Part of Talent Management 16
Near-Term Purposes 16
Longer-Term Purposes 20
Business Situations Related to Assessment 27
The Development of Senior Executives 32
Summary 33

Chapter 3   What to Assess   **35**

Competencies   37
Failure Factors   40
Experience/Previous Results versus Behavioral Style   41
Pulling It All Together   41
Dual Capability   42
Learning Agility   44
Executive Intelligence   45
Emotional Intelligence   45
Relationships as Opposed to Interpersonal Skills   46
A Cautionary Note: The Role of Charisma   46
Toxic Leaders   47
Types of Experience/Previous Results   51
Fit   52
Summary: Determining What to Assess   61
Summary   62

Chapter 4   How to Assess   **65**

The Feel of Senior Executive Assessment   66
Methods   68
Summary   104

Chapter 5   Additional Practical Decisions   **107**

Development Revisited   108
Coaching   109
Other Practical Issues   114
The Future of Senior Executive Assessment   135
Summary   138

Notes   141
References   143
Names Index   145
Subject Index   147

Series Editor's Preface

The *Talent Management Essentials* series presents state-of-the-art thinking on critical talent management topics ranging from global staffing, to career pathing, to engagement, to executive staffing, to performance management, to mentoring, to real-time leadership development. Authored by leading authorities and scholars on their respective topics, each volume offers state-of-the-art thinking and the epitome of evidence-based practice. These authors bring to their books an incredible wealth of experience working with small, large, public and private organizations, as well as keen insights into the science and best practices associated with talent management.

Written succinctly and without superfluous "fluff," this series provides powerful and practical treatments of essential talent topics critical to maximizing individual and organizational health, well-being, and effectiveness. The books, taken together, provide a comprehensive and contemporary treatment of approaches, tools, and techniques associated with Talent Management. The goal of the series is to produce focused, prescriptive volumes that translate the data- and practice-based knowledge of organizational psychology, human resources management, and organizational behavior into practical, "how to" advice for dealing with cutting-edge organizational issues and problems.

Talent Management Essentials is a comprehensive, practitioner-oriented series of "best practices" for the busy solution-oriented manager, executive, HR leader, and consultant. And, in its application of evidence-based practice, this series will also appeal to professors, executive MBA students, and graduate students in Organizational Behavior, Human Resources Management, and I/O Psychology.

Steven G. Rogelberg

Preface

The decisions about which people to put into senior executive jobs are important and difficult. Every CEO with whom I have spoken has a handful of horror stories about being wrong when hiring or promoting individuals into positions involving great responsibility. Organizations approach these critical selection situations in a variety of ways. Often these decisions are based on interviews that do not possess a great deal of rigor. This book makes the case that: (1) for good reasons, there are higher standards than ever before in the area of corporate governance and (2) responsible corporate governance means in part being more thorough and effective in selecting and growing senior executives.

This case needs to be made because the pursuit of responsible corporate governance through senior executive assessment faces roadblocks. While the assessment of employees has become more common in many regions of the world, much of assessment is not done at the highest levels in an organizational structure. I recently was consulting with a $200 billion oil and gas company. They were eager to introduce 360 degree surveys to mid-level management (in this case, to help each individual assessed improve through increased self-awareness). When asked about expanding this assessment to them, the senior executives wanted no part of it. They did not yet realize the strategic and competitive value of effectively conducted executive assessment.

The time is right to inform more CEOs, board members, and other involved parties about useful existing senior executive assessment approaches. This book is meant to be a concise, practical, one-stop "how to" guide that can "demystify" assessment that is conducted at senior executive levels. It includes an assortment of tools, forms, and exercises that can be readily copied or modified for organizational use. "Good to Know" boxes that include summary points are found throughout the book. We also highlight real-world examples and key issues in assessment in "Case Scenario" sections. Finally, each chapter is accompanied by brief introductions and summaries.

CEOs and boards need to know what the options are when introducing assessment. This book is meant to inform buyers and consumers of senior executive assessment, and help them decide which assessment approaches can be the most useful for them. It is written for people who have heard about assessment but do not know a lot about it. This book is different from other sources about assessment in that it expressly is not written for researchers or assessment providers. In summary, the intended audience is:

- CEOs;
- Board members;
- Private equity professionals;
- Enterprise leaders in Human Resources and Talent Management;
- MBA program faculty and students;
- Executive search professionals;
- Senior executives and high potential executives who want to learn about assessment.

Acknowledgments

I would like to start by thanking all of the individuals mentioned in the book who have provided me with their observations about organizations and the role of senior executive assessment. I want to show my appreciation to Steven Rogelberg who edited this series and to Eric Elder for his insightful comments. I want to thank my colleagues Peter Drummond-Hay, Katharine MacLaverty, and Erika Mannion for their input and support. Next, I want to thank Doug Edwards, Darleen DeRosa, and Amy Hayes for their comments throughout the preparation of this book. You all were extremely helpful and central to my efforts. I especially want to emphasize Erin Page's, Stacey Wolman's, and Kathy Schnure's contributions. These three contributed substantially to the chapter summaries and several sections. I also want to thank Laura Bergey for her administrative work (Heather Webb too!), and Kate Nellis and Laura Lydic for their help with research.

Chapter 1

The Case for Senior Executive Assessment

While CEOs and boards undoubtedly realize the importance of hiring for key leadership positions, they are often likely to defer to their subjective opinions and impressions about potential candidates in making such decisions. While this personal experience, intuition, and judgment are useful in the decision-making process, there is little time and resources being invested into services that allow for more objective and systematic appraisals of candidates. The global issue facing executive assessment is twofold. First of all, many CEOs and boards may not even be aware of the options that are available to assist them in the selection process. This lack of awareness is the result of a variety of reasons, many of which boil down to the fact that assessment consultants and firms have had fairly low visibility to date. Second, CEOs and boards may be somewhat skeptical of the executive assessment process in general.

Despite these issues, there is strong evidence that the quality of senior executives has a tangible impact on an organization's performance. The use of senior executive assessment provides a unique platform for addressing critical topics, including personnel selection, mergers and acquisitions, and succession management. Coupled with changes in rules and regulations related to corporate governance, the use of assessment may have added benefit in helping lower corporate risk.

The goal of this chapter is to provide an introduction to senior executive assessment, including the previous obstacles to wide acceptance and potential benefits to organizations that adopt these practices.

Companies know more about their enterprise technology than they do about their enterprise leadership. Many organizations typically expend significant proportions of revenue on testing, introducing, and monitoring their information technology systems. However, they invest less time and resources "getting under the hood" to ensure they have the full picture about the people that actually run (or will run) a given organization.

For example, the installation of enterprise software (such as SAP's systems that monitor finance, manufacturing, distribution, and human resources) often involves one to three years of planning and execution. The introduction of this software is an elaborate process involving extensive testing and retesting. The typical monetary investment for this installation process at a significantly sized company can vary from approximately $1 million to $100 million. Yet the decisions leading to the hiring and promotion of senior executives frequently are made in a far more casual manner (perhaps two days' worth of interviews).

Why is this the case? Why do companies invest more in testing their technology than testing their senior executives? It may be that CEOs and boards want to bring their personal experience and intuition to decisions about senior executives. While they often strive for objectivity and consider data in many business decisions, CEOs and boards are used to using their gut and personal impressions when ultimately making decisions, including decisions about people. For some decision-makers, the unspoken belief is that they will *know* senior leadership assets and liabilities when they see them. They believe they are attending to ethereal qualities that are best detected personally by experienced decision-makers (who will have to live with the decision).

Why CEOs and Boards Tend Not to Know a Lot about Senior Executive Assessment

CEOs and boards either do not know about the assessment options readily available to them, or they are wary of them. The summary in the box below ("Why CEOs and Boards Tend Not to Know a Lot about Senior Executive Assessment") attends to the first part of the problem.

CEOs and boards may have little exposure to assessment methods. Assessment may be known only as pre-employment testing at employee and supervisory levels. However, since 1993 I have asked people whom I am about to interview whether they have ever been through an assessment process previously (for hiring or development, for example). In 1993, approximately 30% of mid-level managers or above told me yes. Fifteen years later, approximately 80% tell me yes. Assessment has been moving up organizational structures through the years. The logical and strategic extension of this trend is that senior executive (and board) assessment will continue to become more common.

In addition, most senior executives have MBAs. Business school served as their introduction to all things important regarding knowledge and tools that were to help executives fulfill their responsibilities and become successful. A casual review of business school curricula yields little content about assessment. Only a handful of programs, such as Case Western Reserve's Weatherhead School of Management, feature assessment overtly.

Also, "employee testing" traditionally has been the domain of Human Resources functional areas. Few CEOs and board members have experienced a rotation through these areas of responsibility. This can also lead to assessment not being "top of mind."

Some important processes, however, do eventually transcend the Human Resources domain. One example is executive compensation. While general employee compensation is still conventionally a part of Human Resources, senior executive compensation often has the attention of CEOs and boards. Therefore, board compensation committees are very active in monitoring and discussing senior executive compensation issues (often through the use of consultants). Senior executive assessment may transcend this Human Resources boundary as well.

Many assessment professionals in the 60s, 70s, and 80s were clinical psychologists. These individuals were practically minded clinicians who wanted to explore a new (and deep-pocketed) client base. Clinical psychologists are trained to use confidentiality in the way they treat information about their clients. This confidentiality extends to the identity of clients. The challenge here is that the cornerstone of most business development in professional services involves demonstrating credibility through the discussion of specific work with specific clients. While people with different backgrounds (education and training) now become experts in senior executive assessment, this clinically based history may hinder the discussion about achievements in assessment conducted in organizations.

Many professional services firms advertise extensively, especially when they believe they can catch the attention of people who are CEOs or who sit on corporate boards. When I watch the Masters or other golf tournaments on television, I am exposed to the names and features of audit, tax, and consulting firms. I have yet to see a television advertisement explicitly about senior executive assessment. The closest advertisement I have seen is a commercial extolling the virtues of assessment as a part of online dating services such as eHarmony!

Senior executive assessment is often a behind-the-scenes activity that serves in support of decisions. It is not flashy or sexy. In that way, again it is a bit like audit or tax consulting. If there was a headline in the newspaper about recent senior assessment triumphs, to be accurate it would read "Board Does Not Consider CEO as a Good Fit Due to Rigorous Interviewing and Sound Testing." Assessment professionals are rarely in the media.

Networking is another way that consultants gain new business at senior levels. My observation is that most assessment professionals are earnest, salt of the earth people. They are often self-reliant, hands-on, and technical professionals who may not hang around senior executives frequently in their spare time. Exposure of senior executive assessment through networking is thus limited.

Many senior executives enter their roles through recruitment by retained search firms who have traditionally not used assessment methods as a part of this process. Therefore, senior-level decision-makers miss an opportunity to be exposed to assessment in many hiring situations. Only within the past five years is there evidence that major and boutique search firms are integrating more rigorous assessment methods into their work. An unscientific review of these firms suggests that recently 25–50% of these search firms have introduced assessment testing and other methods into their assignments.

Finally, some CEOs and boards possess the belief that it is difficult to find quality talent for senior executive positions. Given this assumption of scarcity, the last thing on a decision-maker's mind is to use an assessment process toward the end of an extensive search process to decrease the number of candidates. The reverse is true in assessment at lower levels in an organizational structure. Assessment is used in these instances to bring focus to a large candidate pool.

Summary:
Why CEOs and Boards Tend Not to Know a Lot about Senior Executive Assessment

1. It only recently is becoming more prevalent at the senior-most levels in organizations.
2. It rarely is described in business schools.
3. It primarily is hidden within the human resources function.
4. Part of assessment's heritage is in clinical psychology, and clinicians emphasize confidentiality about clients and tend not to promote themselves.
5. External assessment consultants currently do not advertise broadly.
6. It is rarely mentioned in the media.
7. Many assessment professionals are not "well networked" with CEOs and board members.
8. Senior-level recruiting firms historically have not used rigorous assessment methods.
9. It is difficult enough to find good senior executive candidates – there is no need to assess the few good candidates

Why CEOs and Boards Are Wary of Senior Executive Assessment

Everyone has knick-knacks of some type in their office. These can include photos, paperweights, and even signs bearing messages. I have noticed an interesting trend in signs/messages in CEOs' offices. Many of the best CEOs with whom I have worked feature some message in their office that shows their disdain for excuses. One version has the word "excuses" slashed out with red ink and in a red circle, just like the road signs found especially in Europe. The point is they want to bring as much into their control as is possible to try to ensure success. This is why senior decision-makers may not at first glance want to make use of senior executive assessment. They may feel that it takes the hiring process or a favorite candidate out of their hands, for example.

The cornerstone of effective assessment is accuracy. Yet CEOs and boards may doubt that a set of written questions or a professionally conducted interview can adequately capture the personality and drive of a complex and accomplished person. These critics may be concerned about faking and the distortion of responses on the part of a smart person being assessed who is motivated to show themselves in a positive way. They may believe that assessment methods result in insights that are general and undifferentiated, just like horoscopes and astrology.

Many potential consumers of senior executive assessment are very successful themselves. They either implicitly or explicitly attribute portions of their own success to their effectiveness in reading people. They do not want to believe that they should need help in uncovering limitations in a person or predicting a person's behavior. Taking this point further, when executives make hiring decisions that have poor outcomes, they often attribute this failure to the candidates' inability to perform well and adapt. The thinking is such that the hiring failure is not about the hiring executive. Hiring executives in this situation will therefore see no reason to improve their hiring processes.

A large portion of senior assessment work is conducted by psychologists. The image that many people, not just CEOs and those who sit on boards, have of psychologists is often not favorable. The concerns fall into two categories. One is that they are weird, strange, and offbeat. Therefore, the methods they use are weird, strange, and offbeat. The other is that the process is overly technical and mechanical or overly theoretical. Therefore, the process will not feel like a meeting or conversation, or anything that resembles a day in the life of a senior executive. The concern is that assessment will feel like something being done to senior executives, like a medical procedure.

Given the stereotype that these assessment specialists might be weird, the related concern is that the relationship with an assessment professional might not be enjoyable. Even worse than weird, assessment professionals might be dry, serious, and devoid of a sense of humor. The summary in the box below ("Why CEOs and Boards are Wary of Senior Executive Assessment") summarizes these reasons why CEOs and boards may be wary of senior executive assessment.

What Is Senior Executive Assessment?

Senior executive assessment is a process that introduces rigor and objectivity into the measurement of the current capabilities and/or

Summary:
Why CEOs and Boards are Wary of Senior Executive Assessment

1. They fear that they will have less control or influence over decisions.
2. They are not sure of the accuracy of assessment methods.
3. They believe that they themselves should be completely competent in "reading" people – they are not sure what assessment methods can add to a decision.
4. They have a belief that assessment methods will be too weird, contrived, or uncomfortable for those being assessed.
5. They have a belief that assessment professionals will not be able to build rapport or credibility with those being assessed.

future potential of a senior executive (or group of senior executives). This assessment process can be applied to a vast array of decisions and situations (for example, hiring, promotion, succession, mergers and acquisitions, and private equity) that will be discussed later. The different methodological options (for example, interviews and questionnaires) will also be discussed later. Assessment can be conducted by external consultants or internal colleagues, often from Human Resources. Depending on methodology, the individual conducting assessment work may or may not have a degree in psychology.

While many people use the term "senior executive" in different ways, for the purposes of this book senior executives are defined as chief executive officers and their direct reports in organizations that have revenue of $100 million or above (or in the case of not-for-profit or government organizations, having total annual budgets of $100 million or above). This book will not address a small but growing subset of senior executive assessment – board assessment. Typically, board assessment involves the measurement of the composition and mix of a board in terms of knowledge and skills, largely to ensure compliance to governance rules and parameters (although board directors have been asking me recently and more frequently about measuring the decision-making dynamics and interpersonal functioning of a board).

Senior executive assessment is different from assessment at lower levels in an organizational structure in several ways (see the box "How Senior Executive Assessment Differs from Assessment at Lower Levels in an Organization").

> ## How Senior Executive Assessment Differs from Assessment at Lower Levels in an Organization
>
> 1. CEOs and boards are the decision-making clients.
> 2. Duties and responsibilities of those assessed are broader, more complex, and often more substantial.
> 3. Different characteristics or competencies are important at senior levels (for example, setting strategic direction when faced with ambiguity).
> 4. Many senior executive position descriptions and contexts are unique. Therefore, benchmarking and statistical analysis using large samples can be challenging. A deep understanding of the unique situation is needed.
> 5. As clients, CEOs and boards simultaneously expect both rigor and efficiency in assessment methods and reporting.

The Benefits of Senior Executive Assessment

When initiating the business case for senior-level assessment, one approach is to try to prove what many already believe – that the quality of senior executives matters. For example, a study conducted by Weiner and Mahoney[1] examined 193 companies and concluded that the quality of executives related to 44% of variation in profit margins and 47% of variation in stock prices. On the lower end of the continuum and specific to CEOs, Joyce, Nohria, and Roberson[2] found that who the CEO is relates to 14% of the movement in financial results.

Other researchers have tried to illustrate the impact of senior executives by estimating the cost of senior executive turnover or mismatch to a job. According to some research, approximately one-third of executive promotions and hiring decisions are considered a failure.[3] The total cost of executive turnover or mismatch is estimated to be 18 to 47 times that mismatched executive's total cash compensation.[4] This multiplier is likely larger for senior executives in big organizations.

Large business transactions such as mergers and acquisitions (M&A) or private equity/venture capital (PE/VC) investment often involve extensive analysis (due diligence analysis of financials and business processes) before deals are finalized. The emphasis in most due diligence processes is usually not overtly or specifically on people or leaders (although this is changing). This lack of people due diligence can lead to problems and turmoil. In one VC firm's (middle market, $1.3 billion under management) experience in a two-year period, CEOs were replaced in 59% of their investments. While upgrading CEOs is to be expected in a significant amount of VC situations, 59% is extensive.

Regarding M&A, Harding and Rouse at Bain and Company wrote in a recent *Wall Street Journal* article[5] that:

> Rigorous human due diligence helps acquirers get off to a running start. Having done their homework, the new bosses can uncover capability gaps, as well as diffuse points of friction and differences in decision-making. Most important, when critical people decisions are made right away – who stays, who goes, who runs the combined business – an acquired business is more likely to succeed.

Harding and Rouse found that when they took a look at 40 recent M&A deals, "nearly every" acquirer in the 15 deals labeled as successful identified key individuals for retention during pre-deal due diligence or just after the announcement of the deal. Only one-third of the acquirers in the unsuccessful deals identified key employees for retention.

One can extend this analysis by attempting to measure the value of senior executive assessment itself, not just senior executives. In VC transactions, Smart[6] discovered a strong link between the presence and thoroughness of an executive assessment process and the IRR (institutional rate of return) measuring the effectiveness of deals/ return on deal investment. He found 80% IRRs in situations involving thorough assessment and under 30% IRRs in situations involving little or no assessment.

Assessment is involved in most rigorous corporate succession programs these days (when there are rigorous succession programs). Byham, Smith, and Paese[7] contrasted company results based on whether succession management programs were "strong" versus "less strong or not strong." They found that 22% of companies featuring strong succession management programs in their sample were in the top quintile in annual return. On the other side of the coin, 13% of companies featuring weaker succession management programs in their sample were in the top quintile in annual return.

Besides examining the relationship between assessment and business results, one could look at whether assessment can promote success in the ultimate criterion in business – execution. Larry Bossidy was Chairman and CEO of AlliedSignal (which became $24 billion Honeywell). Bossidy's career included many successes, much of which revolved around improvements in cost savings and productivity. Bossidy's tenure was highlighted by 31 consecutive quarters of earnings-per-share growth of 13% or more, according to his biography on the company's website. He emphasized seven behaviors as being important for execution success in the book *Execution: The Discipline of Getting Things Done*:[8]

1. Know your people and your business.
2. Insist on realism.
3. Set clear goals and priorities.
4. Follow through.
5. Reward the doers.
6. Expand people's capabilities.
7. Know yourself.

I think it is reasonable to assert that assessment serves as a tool with regard to succeeding in four of the seven behaviors: know your people, insist on realism, expand people's capabilities, and know yourself. Indeed, Bossidy frequently has stressed the importance of effective interviewing and referencing of candidates.

One could argue with the details of these different studies and assertions, but in the end the debate may be a waste of time. CEOs and boards either intuitively are confident that having the right leader in the right place at the right time is important, and/or they know that their job is to always obtain as good a person as they practically can for a job.

The real question was voiced to me recently by the Chairman and CEO of a $5 billion industrial company who is facing the challenge of finding his replacement: how much information is needed by CEOs and boards when making senior executive decisions? My answer to this question is one word: more.

New Expectations about Corporate Governance

A new dimension in understanding the case for senior executive assessment relates to the global shift in perspective about corporate governance. The assumptions about the major corporate failures in the United States during the earlier part of this decade are that poor corporate oversight and undesirable characteristics in senior executives were to blame. While much of the Sarbanes–Oxley Act of 2002 (SOX) in the United States is oriented at a granular level toward finance and accounting, the main themes in this legislation are really about corporate responsibility and internal controls. While not all companies technically are subjected to SOX and there is recent evidence that companies are spending less money on it, SOX and similar legislation in other countries has had a large impact on business policies and procedures.

This impact was best summarized to me by the enterprise head of Human Resources in a $10 billion (in assets) insurance company recently. When describing why he wanted to start a senior executive assessment program, he said that his company's board now "feels the fiduciary responsibility to survey the executive landscape." Fiduciary responsibility. Surveying of the executive landscape. This summary aligns with my observation that boards are now driving increased interest about senior executive assessment. Because boards are interested, CEOs and those who lead Human Resources and Talent Management are becoming more interested in senior executive assessment too (and being put in a position of answering questions about it).

From the board member's perspective, there is clear guidance about the importance of assessment from another important source. The Fifth Edition of the *Corporate Director's Guidebook*, published in 2007 by the American Bar Association (ABA), describes the overall responsibilities of board members. While SOX and this ABA book were written specifically for board members of public companies, much of the guidance can be considered relevant for a private company board member – especially if one is a board member of a closely held company considering an initial public offering (IPO) or facing the general market pressure to comply with the spirit and intent of SOX. Two of the six main corporate director responsibilities enumerated by the ABA relate directly to the need for senior executive assessment:

1. "Selecting the CEO, setting the goals for the CEO and other senior executives, evaluating and establishing their compensation, and making changes when appropriate."

2. "Developing, approving, and implementing succession plans for the CEO and top senior executives."

The *Corporate Director's Guidebook* provides further detail about the board member's assessment-related duties on page 87:

> Consequently, the board must select the CEO with care and due consideration for the challenges facing the corporation. Equally important, the board is responsible for monitoring the CEO's performance over time and must determine whether there is a need for a change in senior management, including the CEO, in light of the CEO's performance and the corporation's challenges.

While the need for attention on senior executive selection and succession is clear, board members appear concerned about their ability to follow through effectively in this area. According to the 2003–2004 governance survey by the National Association of Corporate Directors, directors ranked succession planning as their most important issue. These directors also conveyed that succession planning is the area where they are least effective and need the most help. This is a problem that assessment can solve.

In the *Harvard Business Review*, Ram Charan recommended that:

> Senior executive development should be overseen by the board's compensation and organization committee, which needs to receive periodic reports on the entire pool of potential CEOs and regular updates on those bobbing near the top of it. The committee should spend a third of its time examining lists of the top 20 candidates in the leadership pipeline. In addition, at least 15% of the 60 or so hours that members meet as a full board should be devoted to succession. At minimum, the board ought to dedicate two sessions a year to hashing over at least five CEO candidates, both internal and external.[9]

While making senior-level personnel decisions without rigorous and independent assessment processes may not lead to corporate failure, the risks and downsides I have observed are numerous. Assessment will not eliminate risk, but it will decrease it. The ways in which assessment mitigates risk are listed in the box "Ways in which Senior Executive Assessment Mitigates Risk". Board members in all different types of companies are in the risk management business.

Senior executive assessment helps board members and CEOs be informed about the tradeoffs in executive talent beyond what can be seen in casual observation. It helps decision-makers understand how strong a strength is and how weak a weakness is.

Ways in which Senior Executive Assessment Mitigates Risk

1. Increased detail supporting the defensibility of a decision.
2. Increased understanding as to whether an internal executive is better or worse than an executive outside the company. Assessment professionals can often provide different types of benchmarking.
3. Assessment professionals often drive a clearer understanding of what is needed in roles. Without assessment, a decision process often can be laborious, inefficient, and lacking in focus. This is frustrating in general, but especially when assessment-related decisions are in the press/public eye.
4. Ability to challenge assumptions about what is needed in roles. Assessment professionals can help ensure, for example, that there is not an over-emphasis on industry track record and experience when the situation may not call for this background.
5. Effective assessment pushes decision-makers in their thinking about organizational culture and fit. Without assessment, there can be a lack of clarity regarding whether a successful candidate is supposed to blend into an organizational culture, change it, or both.
6. The communication of development feedback during a candidate's transition to a new role. Without this guidance, successful candidates can miss an opportunity to "hit the ground running."

Summary

Although senior executive assessment has not yet gained universal acceptance among the entire population of CEOs and boards, the evidence obtained to date concerning its usefulness and effectiveness is positive and supportive. While companies have historically focused more attention on evaluating their "hard" capital investments than on evaluating their human capital, this orientation is likely to experience a change in focus in the coming years.

The practice of assessment is strategically positioned to address the needs of a rapidly changing economy and workforce. For example, in the face of economic challenges, decisions about personnel selection and promotion are even more critical as companies look inward to maximize the performance of internal talent. Furthermore, the composition of the workforce and the content of work are changing to address globalization and advances in technology. As a result, companies need a systematic method for gauging whether candidates possess the right combination of skills for leading their teams, setting strategy, and driving performance in a dynamic environment.

Finally, given the increasing rigor being imposed in corporate governance, CEOs and boards are becoming more acutely aware of and focused on effective corporate governance. Executive assessment professionals are able to combine a rigorous scientific approach with business acumen and knowledge of the key issues facing senior executives to help maximize opportunities and reduce the risks facing companies.

Chapter 2

Purposes

Senior executive assessment is applicable to a wide range of situations. At a broad level, the goal of senior executive assessment is to answer questions about senior executive talent. The benefit of senior executive assessment is that the approach is highly customizable and can be tailored precisely to answer the questions that a CEO or board is facing at any given time. For example, an executive assessment can be conducted to address near-term issues related to Talent Management, which can include hiring decisions, promotions, and team reviews. Longer-term questions can also benefit from the foresight that comes from an in-depth assessment. Senior executive assessment can be used to guide companies in developing or managing succession plans, during due diligence phases for venture capital and private equity investments, in driving turnarounds, and for other types of projects that necessitate a more forward-looking view.

While assessment is generally considered within the context of decision-making, there is an important developmental component as well. Specifically, assessment projects can help identify the strengths of a senior executive and senior executive team as well as provide areas for development. In addition, assessment consultants are able to apply their experience and knowledge to provide developmental plans for a senior executive.

The purpose of the current chapter is to discuss the importance of senior executive assessment in the context of Talent Management and to describe the wide variety of organizational issues which may necessitate or support the use of an executive assessment.

A Part of Talent Management

At first glance, the term Talent Management is broad, amorphous, and smacks of "business speak." Nonetheless, once understood, it is a useful concept in summarizing a major aspect of a CEO's responsibilities and a central portion of the Human Resources function's activities. In fact, *The Economist* magazine found that CEOs in companies of $1 billion or more in revenue often spend more than 20% of their time on Talent Management.

Talent Management starts with the recognition that the knowledge, skills, abilities, and competencies of the people in an organization are important to the results in that organization. Therefore, it behooves the organization to ensure that the supply and quality of talent are at acceptable levels. The supply and quality are ensured through the effective oversight of talent in each stage of its passage and presence in the organization (recruiting, hiring, learning, promotion, succession, performance management, exiting). Assessment is a practical tool that allows for the clear oversight and monitoring of the supply and quality of talent.

There are many potential purposes or situations that call for senior executive assessment. These purposes involve different situations with their own needs, but they all are similar in that decision-makers have questions that need answering about key senior executive talent.

Near-Term Purposes

Hiring

Hiring assessment is focused on gaining more information about the fit between external candidates and the requirements involved in an open position. It is best applied when the selection process is 75–80% complete, when one or several finalists have been chosen, and when there is still one more round of interviewing or another contact point scheduled between candidates and decision-makers. Hiring assessments often resemble fire drills because this finalist phase often sneaks up on a selection process and no one wants to lose a "warm" candidate due to delay in the process – so the scheduling of a hiring assessment can be challenging and frenetic.

A supplementary purpose for many hiring assessments is to facilitate and accelerate the effective entry of a successful candidate into a new organization. This work is often called onboarding or assimilation. The assumption behind this work is that many new senior executives can benefit from guidance about their behavior in the new organization as well as guidance about a company's culture and how things get done within that organization. Researchers such as John Gabarro and Michael Watkins have written extensively about the importance of a successful candidate approaching their first weeks and months in a thoughtful and informed way. Input from onboarding assessment can also go to the manager of the newly hired senior executive, helping them understand how to best manage, communicate with, and motivate the new senior executive.

Promotions

Promotion situations are similar to hiring situations in that there is a current and existing opening, but different in that internal candidates are being considered. Because this group is more "captive" than external candidates, the logistics involved in scheduling promotion assessments are less frenetic than hiring situations. However, egos and existing relationships are very important to manage in promotion assessment situations. The danger of departure in unsuccessful candidates or candidates who are not considered for promotion is significant. Assessment does help ensure that internal candidates are considered thoroughly and fairly. In a related way, assessment can help promote the assets of an internal candidate that are not well known.

External and Internal Candidate "Hybrid" Situations

More organizations are asking about the simultaneous or near-simultaneous assessment of both external and internal candidates at senior levels. In this way, a decision-maker can feel peace of mind that he or she is maximizing the probability of introducing the best available talent into an open job. Therefore, a CEO can consider the benefits and problems in introducing a completely new leader to the organization side by side with the benefits and problems of choosing an internal candidate who possesses useful institutional knowledge and fit to the current organizational culture.

Internal and external candidates can be considered in parallel and simultaneously if the selection decision is urgent and the organization is at that time willing to invest in an external search. Internal and external candidates can be considered in sequence if the decision is not urgent. I often recommend that internal senior candidates are assessed at least two years before a selection decision is projected to occur, for two reasons: to allow internal candidates time to develop based on recommendations from the assessment and to allow any subsequent external search an appropriate amount of time. Many senior-level executive searches take between three and six months.

Another supplementary benefit of the assessment and development of internal candidates is that the process can help the organization retain internal candidates while they are being considered for a job and even after they have been turned down on occasion. The assessment process and the subsequent development process keep the senior executive talent engaged and involved in the organization. The organization pays attention to and invests in these individuals during assessment. I currently have one technology client that is facing great change and turmoil and has reported that the assessment program has in itself served as a retention tool.

In summary, assessments involving both internal and external candidates clarify each candidate's strengths and areas for concern. An example of this process is provided in the Case Scenario below.

Case Scenario:
External and Internal
Candidate Assessment

Situation: The client was a large, not-for-profit organization. For most of this organization's senior roles, there were both internal and external candidates under consideration, and there was a need for an objective evaluation of the individuals' experience and leadership potential. First, candidates met with search consultants and completed standard competency-based interviews in order to quickly reach a short list. The assessment process then began for each of the short-list candidates. They completed psychometric tests measuring personality and cognitive ability, and then participated in behavioral interviews with our assessment consultants.

Result: The assessment work helped to differentiate between candidates with comparable levels of experience, and the client was better able to make informed selection decisions, including the promotion of an internal candidate. Additionally, comprehensive development suggestions were given to each of the internal candidates.

While I have frequently seen CEOs and boards debate the relative merits of "going outside" versus "going inside," I rarely see a thoughtful and systematic treatment of the subject. However, George Anders wrote a practical article on the subject in the *Wall Street Journal*. The article cites that for every General Electric that uses internal candidates to fill approximately 80% of senior executive openings, there is a Cisco Systems that uses internal candidates to fill approximately 60% of senior executive openings. Anders summarized that while certain organizations will have their internal or external leanings, the presence or absence of the business situations in the Tips box below (along with an overall shortage of available internal talent or insufficient succession planning processes) should lead an organization to decide when to go to the outside in a more coherent way.

Tips:
Factors Leading to the Pursuit of
External Senior Executive Candidates

1. Geographic expansion in which no internal talent can fit the geography
2. Fast moving, new lines of business and rapid growth
3. Need for new areas of functional expertise
4. Organizational change
5. Repeated problems in an area of responsibility in which internally sourced talent has been unsuccessful

---

Senior Executive Team Reviews

This type of talent review or inventory involves gaining a current analysis of the strengths and weaknesses of an intact and already existing senior executive group. The assumption is that by identifying and then filling gaps, the group's functioning and therefore the organization's performance will improve. Gaps identified could be in areas such as functional expertise, strategic approach, or tactical approach. Bob McGehee, the former Chairman and CEO of Progress Energy, summarized this type of work this way to me: "the assessment gave us a solid understanding of where we need deeper talent levels and where we have talent that requires special retention consideration." This type of assessment usually is done such that there is a "snapshot" of the overall group measured in one intensive time period, perhaps three months. I have been a part of team reviews that were conducted with four executives assessed in a $100 million company and a team review of over 100 executives in a $100 billion international retailer.

A classic situation that leads to a team review is the arrival of a new CEO. While some CEOs will want to be completely independent in developing their point of view about their inherited senior executive team, many wish to complement their own thinking and accelerate their insights by conducting a senior executive assessment exercise at some point in the first 12 months of their tenure.

Longer-Term Purposes

The near-term purposes described above were such that the focus was on creating insight into a senior executive's current capabilities. Along a continuum, assessment also can contribute insight about an executive's future capabilities, or potential. While assessing potential is often part of the assessment work I just described, it is more explicitly important in the contexts below.

Succession Management

Succession management periodically receives attention in the business press. This area especially receives focus when there are broader forces that cause the demise of multiple CEOs. For example, during the 2008 sub-prime mortgage lending crisis in the United States, the business press has sought to emphasize the lack of succession planning following the ousting of CEOs in several large financial institutions (Citigroup, Merrill Lynch). The business press again was surprised that many large organizations do not have formal succession plans in place.

The succession management process seeks to identify future leadership gaps within an organization and create plans to ensure leadership stability, with considerable focus being placed on the identification of high-potential executive talent. Assessment is commonly used to identify these high-potential individuals who will eventually fill key roles within an organization.

Succession management in detail is beyond the scope of this book. Assessment's role, however, is brought alive when I describe the broader context and process. I often recommend that designing an organization's succession management approach begins with the following. In terms of CEO succession specifically, key members of the board (for example, non-executive Chairman, lead director, head of Compensation Committee, head of Nominations and Governance Committee) are asked an appropriate subset of the questions immediately below:

1. Solicit the CEO's and Human Resources leader's responses to the following diagnostic questions:
   - What is the actual rate at which you fill executive positions internally?
   - What is your target for the rate at which you fill executive positions internally?
   - To what extent do you want diversity to play a role in your succession processes?
   - To what extent do you want the people on succession lists to know that they are on these lists?
   - To what extent do you want others in the organization to know who is on succession lists?
   - What is the extent to which you actually use an internal successor list when there is an executive opening?
   - What is the desired scope for your succession plan? Which positions, functions, and locations do you want to be involved?
   - What are the main elements of your corporate strategy? What are the main implications of this strategy for executive competencies?
   - What is the major timeframe for succession?
2. Design/execute periodic nomination process for internal candidates.
3. Periodically assess internal candidates.
4. Develop/update depth charts for all positions.
5. Design/execute performance and development review process of candidates.
6. Develop/maintain succession information system/summary.
7. Identify trends in areas for development across the group of executives that have been assessed. Implement any necessary group-level development activities.

8. Construct and follow up on development plans for each individual executive.

The main application of assessment in succession management is in providing input about a subset of individuals who are estimated to be the future leaders in a company, usually identified by a nominating group of senior-most executives. This work is different from promotion assessment in that with succession assessment a prospective job is not open, the expected timeframe for an assessed individual to take on a new role is about one year or greater, often an assessed individual is being considered for a pool of future roles and not just one specific job, and often an assessed individual is being evaluated against a core set of executive-level competencies and not just one job's specifications. The following example in Figure 2.1 (all names in this figure and other figures in this book are fictional) shows how a group of executives' performance and potential may be depicted in a succession management report. Some organizations use a performance and potential two-factor matrix approach like the one included in this figure. Other organizations are being more progressive by also taking into account behavioral style in this type of summary table. In this way, the analysis is not only about results and potential, but also whether an individual is a good leader as he or she achieves.

Example: potential and performance in succession management
Besides potential itself, succession management oriented assessment often aims to describe an assessed individual's readiness (ready now, ready in one year, etc.) to take on a new role, as well as mobility (interest and ability in relocating). Figures 2.2 and 2.3 depict two examples of the same type of chart that can be used to summarize information within key succession variables. Boards especially find this summary "dashboard" format useful.

Succession plans may also highlight "exposure" or risk in the senior executive team assessed. Exposure is defined as a problem area that needs to be discussed by the board and/or executive committee because of: (1) the criticality of a position; (2) the absence of any known succession candidates for a critical position; (3) the departure risk of an incumbent; (4) the existence of a problem performer that may require action. An example of a succession management chart that includes exposure is found in Figure 2.4.

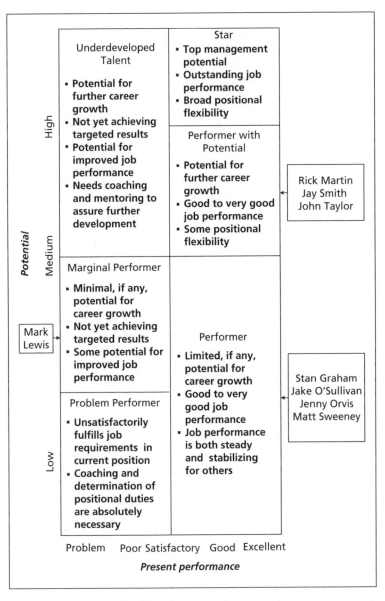

Figure 2.1 Potential and performance in succession management

Competency Ratings (Scale of 1–5)								
Integrity	Stewardship	Business Acumen	Organization Development	Teamwork/ Collaboration	Global Perspective	Innovation	Commitment to Excellence	Average
5	5	4	4	4	4	3	4	4.1

Benchmarking Rating (Scale of 1–4)		Potential Rating (Scale of 1–4)	
4	One of the best candidates possible	4	High Potential/Upside

Key Style Insights/Benchmarking Rationale

Warm, involves himself in a breadth of activities, may sometimes have time management challenges, his self-confidence can be surprisingly low on occasion, outgoing and maintains relationships, sometimes may change decisions or delay decisions, and facilitative.

Possesses useful levels of direct consumer experience and strong general management experience. He also has global experience overall as well as marketing and commercial acumen. He has a diverse functional background and appears able to facilitate growth and innovation. He is light in packaging experience and could use more Asia experience.

Proposed Next Roles	Proposed Next Roles from Individual Assessed	Proposed Next Roles from References
Manage multiple business units (1–2 years), CEO (4–5 years)	New acquisitions role with European exposure, would want to be considered for CEO (3 years)	Group leadership role (1–2 years), lead a new business segment (now), President (2 years), CEO (3–4 years)

Stated Relocation Preferences

2 years from now he will be open to relocation either domestically or internationally.

Potential Derailers/Development Priorities

He needs to deepen packaging experience and show clear wins, ensure he demonstrates effective decisiveness and confidence in key situations.

Risk of Departure/Difficulty in Replacement

Low risk of departure in that he is challenged now and engaged. Difficulty to replace him is high. He possess unique consumer experience that is difficult to attract to a primarily industrial company.

Figure 2.2 Matt Carter, Senior Vice President, Consumer Solutions Group, Company ABC

Competency Ratings (Scale of 1–5)								
Integrity	Stewardship	Business Acumen	Organization Development	Teamwork/ Collaboration	Global Perspective	Innovation	Commitment to Excellence	Average
4	4	4	4	2	2	3	5	3.5

Benchmarking Rating (Scale of 1–4)		Potential Rating (Scale of 1–4)	
4	One of the best candidates possible	3	Moderate Potential/Upside

Key Style Insights/Benchmarking Rationale

Directive, dominant, active critical thinker, seeks variety, oriented to detail, can be intense, vigilant and distrusting on occasion, and possesses a strong focus on career advancement.

He possesses strong business acumen and deep financial knowledge and experience. He possesses an especially strong Street and investor focus. He has real zeal for operational excellence and also appears to have a strong M&A acumen. He appears more turnaround oriented than growth oriented and his success and track record in the past have been more tactical than strategic. He also possesses limited general management experience.

Proposed Next Roles	Proposed Next Roles from Individual Assessed	Proposed Next Roles from References
A business unit President (now), President/COO (1–2 years)	President/COO (now), CEO (2 years)	Run Specialty Chemicals (now), General Manager of a large division, COO (now), CEO (now–3 years), with some people feeling that he might not match the roles as well

Stated Relocation Preferences

Not now, maybe in 2 years either domestically or internationally.

Potential Derailers/Development Priorities

Needs to ensure that he knows when and how to curtail his abrupt, agent of change oriented style.

Risk of Departure/Difficulty in Replacement

High risk of departure given he is very ambitious and is eager to understand whether he is under consideration for CEO and in what amount of time. Difficulty of replacement is low given there are other strong internal candidates for his role and that there should be no issue in attracting an equal caliber of talent from the market.

Figure 2.3 Mike Ross, Senior Vice President, Company ABC

Executive Team

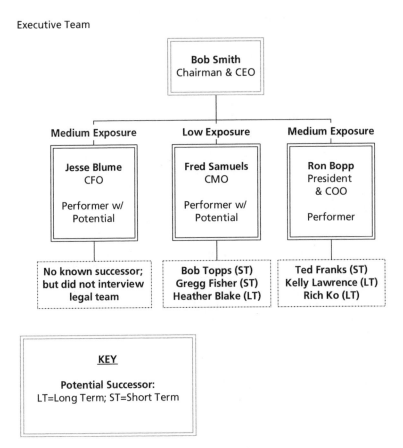

Figure 2.4 A succession management chart with exposure

In this case, two parts of the organization possess exposure to risk. The CFO role is labeled at medium risk because there is no known internal successor to the current CFO. The President and COO role is designated medium risk because the incumbent has been labeled a Performer who by definition does not possess extensive potential to be promoted. Yet there is one internal candidate who has been evaluated as possessing short-term readiness to be promoted. If the organization does not in some way attend to this high-potential talent (effective career planning discussions, for example), this individual may feel "stuck" behind a lesser talent and depart the organization unexpectedly.

Example: succession plan with exposure
Given the nature of succession management, external assessment providers often enter multi-year consulting arrangements with companies that desire succession guidance. The Case Scenario below includes an example of this type of situation.

Case Scenario:
Succession Management

Situation: The ownership group desired an informed perspective on the quality and consistency of talent throughout the subsidiaries, as well as the need to develop more defined succession alternatives globally. We proactively engaged the client in a discussion about how an assessment could inform their succession management decisions.

Result: We presented a thorough evaluation of individual and team capabilities and discussed possible succession plans. We also provided personal feedback to every executive assessed, and they all now have detailed professional development plans. Also, a number of key leadership gaps were identified and we were asked to assess subsequent external candidates given our insight about and understanding of their culture and leadership needs. By now, over 100 executives in the Americas have been assessed in multiple phases and we were recently asked to conduct assessments during recent acquisitions.

Although succession assessment is most often beneficial for both organizations and the individuals within organizations, internal participants are sometimes hesitant to accept assessment. Human Resources professionals at Pepsi have presented solutions to combat employee fear and discomfort with succession assessment.[1] It was suggested that the following are crucial to helping executives see the benefit of succession assessment and for promoting its use:

1. Ensure the framework is clear and understandable.
2. Create a positive mindset regarding assessment. Emphasize development purposes, for example.

3. Introduce executive coaches for development when appropriate. Executive coaches are often beneficial after assessments are completed in helping high-potential talent focus on key development areas. Coaches also represent tangible follow-up about issues identified during assessment.

Business Situations Related to Assessment

Venture Capital (VC) and Private Equity (PE)

VC and PE firms invest large amounts of money into companies of various sizes and stages. VC situations involve early stage, relatively small companies. It is becoming more common for the investors in a VC firm to use assessment to understand the quality of a CEO (and perhaps several others on the management team) of a portfolio company either before or after these professionals invest in the company. Sometimes assessment is bundled into the pre-investment due diligence process, usually after the letter of intent has been signed and finalized. Because the due diligence phase is often compressed in time, the scheduling of this type of assessment usually involves aggressive timeframes.

As with hiring assessment, those who conduct a VC assessment process in a due diligence phase need to ensure they are rigorous and effective in doing the work while simultaneously establishing good rapport so as to not threaten the decision (in this case, the investment decision) that is in process. Also, similar to hiring assessment, reports and debriefing formats in VC due diligence work need to be clear, well substantiated, and business focused.

Assessment is also used to help the VC investors (who also often serve as board members) understand how to best work with the individuals assessed after the investment occurs as all parties attempt to accelerate and maximize the value of the company. Usually one to five individuals are assessed in VC contexts.

In general, PE assessment can serve the same purposes as with VC assessment, but the work is conducted with larger, more established companies. Therefore, the number of individuals assessed in PE situations is usually greater than the number of individuals assessed in VC situations.

When introducing senior executive assessment to VC and PE firms, the items in the "Role of/Reason for Senior Executive Assessment in VC/PE Situations" box have helped VC/PE investors understand the role that assessment can play. Not surprisingly, many of these same messages can be used in corporate settings.

Role of/Reason for Senior Executive Assessment in VC/PE Situations

1. Assessment does not replace investors' role in assessing talent; assessment adds to and challenges the insights that are developing about a portfolio management team.
2. Assessment consultants can be used when investors cannot give assessment enough time.
3. Assessment consultants can be used when a VC/PE firm desires deeper assessment expertise than the VC/PE firm has available in-house.
4. Assessment can be used as a common practice within the deal or transaction process, similar to legal and financial services that are commonly used.
5. Assessment can attend specifically to calibrating the seriousness of identified concerns, as well as identifying new risk factors.
6. Assessment can be used to confirm or refute a specific concern about an individual, especially when there is disagreement among investors in the same firm or among investors in two or several co-investing firms.
7. Assessment can be used when an investment is particularly important or sizable.
8. Assessment provides data-based insight that can be useful when communicating and substantiating tough messages about the status of the business and improvement.
9. Assessment can be used when there is need to have a very precise understanding in a particular functional area (for example, financial discipline or sales).

An example that highlights the benefits of PE assessment is the project described in the box below involving a midsized private equity firm that focuses on investing in underperforming companies (see Case Scenario "Private Equity Due Diligence").

Case Scenario:
Private Equity Due Diligence

Situation: A PE firm had recently purchased a company with significant, recent declines in profitability. They suspected that the founders and existing management team could not effectively manage the growth and performance of this now large and complex business. The PE firm sought counsel regarding a plan to quickly realign and re-staff the organization. The project involved the assessment of 15 executives, including the two founders.

Result: As a result of the assessments, we presented a thorough evaluation of individual and team capabilities with a focus on the ability of the assessed executives to restructure and profitably grow the business. In our view, about half of the existing management team were in positions that exceeded their capabilities. Of equal significance, they seemed capable of only viewing the business in the way it had been conducted in the past and could not envision new and different approaches. Consequently, the PE firm agreed, and released about half of the leadership team, including the two founders, and recruited a new CEO, COO, and CFO. The leadership structure was also reorganized to conform to what is typically seen in similar companies in their industry. One year later, the struggling company's operating income had increased 50%.

The purpose of VC/PE assessment is usually to evaluate the quality of a portfolio management team along with providing input into development. Many of these projects are driven by the investment professionals in the VC/PE firms. Understandably, portfolio management can be a particularly anxious group of assessees. As will be discussed later regarding virtually all assessment situations, we especially encourage very clear decision-making and communication about which VC/PE investment professionals will see assessment reports and the timing of who sees assessment reports first – the VC/PE firm or portfolio managers. I have seen this vary greatly depending on the relationship between investors and management, as well as depending on who is paying for the assessment.

Mergers and Acquisitions (M&A)

The intensity of M&A activity will wax and wane. Of course, much of M&A activity is related to the dynamics in a specific market, industry, or sector. Recent overall activity has spiked tremendously – there was $3.8 trillion in M&A volume in 2006. Depending on criteria, roughly 50% of company mergers will fail (interestingly, this percentage is similar to the failure rate of two other types of mergers – the hiring merger mentioned earlier that occurs when a new senior executive joins an organization and a marriage merger when a husband and wife join in wedlock!). Many who analyze such company merger failures, such as Harding and Rouse, have concluded that "people problems are at the root of many failed mergers."

Similar to VC and PE contexts, senior executive assessment in M&A can serve both the before-transaction phase (pre-combination due diligence) and the after-transaction phase (post-combination integration). At the core of the integration assessment work is the comparison and contrast of two or several senior executives for a position in the new, combined entity. While politics and negotiated commitments often enter into the selection decision-making at the highest levels of an organization chart, assessment is used frequently as well (especially when there is a desire to reduce the impact of politics or make the process agnostic regarding an individual's history with one legacy organization or another). Clarifying the ambiguity of who will have what job appears to help company combinations. Therefore, speed and conducting assessment early in the process is important.

Combining measurement rigor with respectfulness is important for all assessment, but especially when an individual may lose a job based in part on the outcome. One example of feedback that helped me gauge to what extent I had treated an assessed candidate respectfully was an offhanded comment from a person I had just interviewed. He was a senior legal executive whom I was assessing in a M&A situation. He knew, and we discussed, how the assessment would have bearing on whether he would be able to retain his senior role in a large, newly combined natural resources company. He was clearly prickly at first. Did I mention he was a lawyer? But at the end of the interview, he felt the need to thank me because he felt that, to use his words, he "had his fair day in court." This comment summarizes the objective for M&A senior executive assessment.

Turnaround

Turnarounds commonly are run by tough people. Yet I am surprised continually by aggressive turnaround CEOs (and private equity investment professionals) who desire data-based insights about key senior executives to help them convey difficult messages about the need for improvement and potential actions. Through assessment, the CEO knows how to best position executive talent for success and how to best work with them in accomplishing turnaround goals.

Performance Improvement

I have also conducted a lot of senior executive assessment work where the context was performance improvement but the organization was not in need of a dramatic turnaround. In this latter situation, CEOs wanted to conduct assessment because it was their feeling that the organization was "not hitting on all cylinders." To use Jim Collins' terminology, they wanted to go "from good to great."

Change in Markets and Business Models

Significant shifts in markets and business models can require a change in the characteristics needed in senior executives. CEOs and boards may therefore want to take a more systematic inventory about their current senior executive talent in an attempt to understand what they have that can match the new situation and what new executive talent will be needed. Examples of these broader shifts are listed in the box below.

Market and Business Model Shifts that may Require Changes in Senior Executive Talent

1. Rapid globalization of an industry
2. Privatization
3. Deregulation
4. Spin off
5. Reorganization

The Development of Senior Executives

While development has been mentioned as a part of other assessment situations, assessment can be conducted for purely developmental purposes as well. For example, the peers and direct reports who work with a CFO can complete a 360 degree survey so they all can describe the CFO at work and in leadership situations. That CFO might receive an assessment report that clarifies his or her strengths, areas for development, and a list of potential development actions. In this scenario, it is common that no one else in the organization has access to the CFO's assessment report except the CFO.

The other extreme can also occur. There are some assessment programs that include primarily an evaluative component. In this case, the senior-most decision-makers see the assessment report, experience an assessment presentation, and use this information subsequently for decisions.

I do not advocate this exclusively evaluative approach. Most organizations understandably want to get more out of their assessment investment than just evaluation. In addition, I believe (and most psychologists who conduct assessment also believe) that people are owed some type of feedback or debriefing about their assessment. I often say that all senior executive assessments are developmental assessments, at least in part.

Examples of this include hiring assessment that becomes onboarding assessment and succession assessment that is also a development assessment. Conger and Fulmer wrote in a seminal *Harvard Business Review* article[2] about executive succession that a fundamental rule in succession management is that it should be married to leadership development. They argued that by connecting both succession planning and leadership development, more attention is paid to identifying the skills required for senior executive positions and a corresponding development approach can be customized to reflect these skills.

It has also been my team's experience that one of the greatest benefits of succession assessment is the identification of crucial areas that potential successors need to develop. Assessment allows for the detection of a successor's potential (that is, the underlying attributes that make someone capable of fulfilling a role), as well as the key skills that need to be developed in order to capitalize on that potential.

In conclusion, senior executive assessment is a tool that can be applied to many business situations. Further, given the complexity involved at senior levels in business today, it is common to have several of these scenarios and purposes operating within one organizational situation.

Summary

The benefit of senior executive assessment is that it does not involve a pre-packaged solution to a company's problems. It is a set of processes, based on established principles and methods, that can be uniquely and specifically combined depending on the purposes at hand.

The key message in this chapter is that executive assessment projects can be undertaken for a very wide variety of reasons and purposes. Executive assessment projects can be used to solve near-term issues such as hiring, promotion decisions, and team reviews. Alternately, they can be used to anticipate and plan for longer-term issues such as succession management, due diligence for venture capital and private equity investments, and in preparing for and driving turnarounds.

Talent Management is based on the notion that the knowledge, skills, abilities, and competencies of an organization's human capital are a critical component of the organization's performance and success. As a result, ensuring that the right people are being hired and promoted into the right jobs should be a primary focus of an organization. Assessment professionals understand this need and are able to use objective measurement to provide rigorous and systematic comparisons between candidates.

Chapter 3

What to Assess

While the benefits and uses of senior executive assessment have now been described, the specific processes involved are less clear. That is, what exactly is being measured in a senior executive assessment? What qualities or skills are being assessed? Assessment professionals have to work to balance the factors that are robust indicators of high-potential talent across situations with the factors that are specific to each business situation.

Competencies are broad constructs or qualities that have been determined to be important for success in an organization. In an assessment project, these competencies are selected to represent the specific demands of a particular organization or position. As a result, candidates can be systematically compared regarding their relative strengths and weaknesses. Failure factors or derailers have also been identified as a critical aspect of what should be assessed. These factors, when identified as characteristics of a candidate, serve as a warning or red flag that the candidate might possess qualities or traits that may be detrimental to the effective functioning of the organization.

Assessment professionals tend to focus on the behavioral qualities and characteristics that are indicative of successful or poor performance. In contrast, traditional executive recruiters have tended to focus on objective business criteria such as experience and proven results. While an assessment professional can shed light on the behavioral or leadership style of candidates, the recruiter tends to ascertain whether candidates have proven themselves and their potential. Both of these perspectives are important to senior executive talent management decisions. It is important to give proper attention to all of these factors.

The purpose of this chapter is to elaborate on the assessment process and to provide detailed information on the "what" of senior executive assessment. Specifically, what factors or qualities are important when assessing senior executives.

When one looks at the business section in an online or bricks-and-mortar bookstore, it becomes abundantly clear that many of the books available are about the "secret" or newly discovered factors related to success in business. Several items need to be considered when going down this path. First, some of this content is really about success in life and not success in an organizational context. Second, some of this material is really about factors leading to business success, but not really about management and leadership. Third, this material can be about leading people and leadership, but not include the full breadth and level involved in senior executive jobs. Fourth, even if the material is about factors needed to run a company, they can be skewed toward being a founding entrepreneur and not a senior corporate leader. Finally, some of this content can confuse what it takes to be promoted into a senior job as opposed to factors that predict success once one is in a senior executive position. I call these books "leadership recipe" books, and there are a lot of them out there.

It is also important to keep in mind that it is useful to pursue a group of factors that remain quite consistent across senior executive situations while simultaneously attending to the fact that each business situation is different. There are enough behavioral themes in senior executive jobs such that we should be able to isolate what is important in many, if not most, senior executive positions. However, I think it is silly to lean on these factors only. In fact, I think far more attention needs to be paid to getting under the surface of current and future organizational strategies and needs, in an attempt to more accurately take into account the situation that the senior executive will face. We need to be far more proactive and discerning during this situational analysis. Later I will isolate the main situational factors and provide guidance about how to probe into the context the senior executive will face.

The factors to be assessed can take on three forms: general "buckets" or categories, success factors, or failure factors. Most psychologists in the 60s, 70s, and 80s used general categories to organize their measurement and reporting about individuals in organizations. These consulting firms and independent practitioners were similar to each other in the format they used for their measurement and reporting. For example, they measured the categories of: emotional factors, social factors, judgment and decision-making, and work style. But the content was not always specific and focused on what related to success and failure. For example, the report might have had a paragraph describing an electric utility executive candidate's overall behavior in communicating with others, but the content might not have been directed at describing the candidate's specific style in communicating with key community, governmental, and regulatory entities.

Competencies

David McClelland primarily started the ball rolling with competencies in the early 70s. Competencies or success factors subsequently developed a lot of momentum in the 80s and 90s. While many stories exist about what was related to this surge of interest, one credible story was conveyed to me by Jim Williams, who is a partner in charge of portfolio company recruitment and hiring at the large private equity firm TPG (formerly Texas Pacific Group).

Earlier in his career Jim and a team of others were attempting to guide Kaiser Permanente, the medical managed care organization, through geographical expansion and extensive combinations with other companies. The company also felt the need to attend to operating losses in some parts of the organization and to shore up quality of care. As a part of this effort, Jim and others created new success factors to specify what was needed in managers and executives to help grow the organization. Around this time, McBer & Company also had conducted many projects demonstrating that competency measurement could predict success in senior executives.

More recently, Michael Lombardo and Bob Eichinger have conducted extensive research on management and executive-related competencies. They have developed a large set of competencies that are organized into different clusters. These competencies can form the structure that not only lies underneath assessment at different levels of an organization, but also can be connected to other facets of talent management (such as learning and performance management). An example of one of their clusters is Making Complex Decisions and an example of an underlying competency in this area is Learning On The Fly.

Many executive assessments are structured around competencies that are tailored to the demands of the organization or situation. The individuals being assessed can then be compared to one another against these competencies using numerical ratings, which are typically based on behaviorally anchored rating scales (i.e., scales that provide descriptive behaviors for different levels of effectiveness). An example of this comparison is found in Table 3.1. It is important to note that often the value added from competency-based assessment comes from the written prose or competency descriptions for each assessee, and not only the numerical values assigned. The numerical ratings provide one efficient way (but only one way) of comparing individuals or groups of individuals with regard to the competencies needed for success.

Example: Competency Comparisons

It has been my team's experience that tables with numerical competency comparisons, such as the example provided in Table 3.1, are extremely helpful when conducting hiring projects. Simple tables that allow decision-makers to better understand the candidates' relative strengths and weaknesses are typically well received. As you can see in Table 3.1, we will sometimes include each person's unweighted average across all the competency scores that allows for the candidates to be ranked.

One advantage of competency ratings is that numerical profiles can be empirically developed for specific positions that capture scoring patterns that result in strong performance. For example, the benchmark competency rating averages for chief operating officers (COOs) in an industrial setting might be in the excellent range in the competencies of Driving Results and Analytical Skill but in the sufficient range in Setting Strategy and Building Relationships. Many organizations and consultancies have developed proprietary competency scoring patterns that relate to success for key types of positions.

The use of the terms competency and competencies has exploded over the past 10 years. At the very least, the benefit of this has been a

Table 3.1 Team competency ratings

	Integrity	Stewardship	Business Acumen	Organization Development	Teamwork / Collaboration	Global Perspective	Innovation	Commitment to Excellence	AVERAGE
Luther, Jeremy	4	4	4	4	4	4	5	4	4.1
Stephens, Peter	4	4	4	4	4	4	4	4	4.0
Yen, Lucy	4	3	4	4	4	4	3	4	3.8
Clark, Jay	3	4	4	4	3	4	3	5	3.8
Martin, Jerry	4	3	4	4	3	4	4	3	3.6
Morris, Matt	4	5	4	3	2	3	2	4	3.4
Klein, John	3	3	2	4	5	3	3	4	3.4
Ross, David	5	4	3	2	2	3	3	3	3.1
Rivers, David	3	3	2	4	4	3	4	2	3.1
Silvers, Fred	2	3	3	4	5	2	3	3	3.1
Carey, Gary	3	2	2	3	4	1	3	2	2.5
AVERAGE:	3.5	3.5	3.3	3.6	3.6	3.2	3.4	3.5	

Rating Scale:
1: Significant Area for Development
2: Area for Development
3: Sufficient
4: Good
5: Excellent

focus on identifying the core factors that lead to success in different positions. At the worst, as with many popular business topics, the concept has been overused and over-applied. I have seen organizations become weighed down by having to sift through dozens of competencies. The enterprise head of Human Resources for Nokia told me several years ago that he did not believe there is one magic set of competencies for executives. It was at that point of our meeting that we discussed the importance of minimizing derailers or failure factors.

Failure Factors

Failure factors started to receive attention in the late 90s. Bob and Joyce Hogan, two active and influential leadership researchers, created a personality inventory that measured characteristics that "derailed" individuals involved in management and executive positions. The major U.S. corporate failures several years later added momentum to this topic. David Dotlich and Peter Cairo,[1] and Sydney Finkelstein,[2] have each written books about senior executive-level failure factors. Patrick Lencioni[3] has also written a book about "The Five Dysfunctions of a Team" which can be applied to senior executive team dynamics.

Many of the failure factors are related to excessive ego. Dealing with excessive egos is a reality amongst the senior executives within many organizations. Organizations may find it useful to learn some lessons from the New England Patriots, now one of the most successful franchises in the history of the National Football League. Their regular season record in 2000 was 5 wins and 11 losses. They then made a significant senior executive change by hiring Bill Belichick as their Head Coach. Since Belichick's hiring, the team has performed well. During his tenure up until the end of 2007, the team has won 86 games and lost 26 in the regular season. They have won the Super Bowl three times as well.

When I discussed the Patriots' philosophy and culture with Thomas Dimitroff, a key figure in the general management structure of the organization, he emphasized several items: (1) eliminate complacency, (2) eliminate entitlement, and (3) ensure people understand and appreciate their specific, well-defined roles. Similarly, Tim Layden of *Sports Illustrated* wrote an article about the selflessness and the "no egos allowed" culture entitled "And One For All."[4] The article states that while these notions are not new, the Patriots have executed well in this area. Not surprisingly, it starts at the top. Team owner Robert Kraft described it explicitly in the *Sports Illustrated* piece when he said "we try to get people who subjugate their egos." Jabar Gaffney, a player on the 2007 team, described it as "no foolishness – nobody is bigger than the team." Another player on the 2007 team, Stephen Neal, said "nobody takes credit. If you say, look what I did, there's a target on your chest." Layden summarizes insightfully that this "atmosphere" causes the organization to be "impervious to distraction." While the Patriots (and other organizations) are successful for a variety of reasons, minimizing the impact of excessive egos appears to help.

Experience/Previous Results versus Behavioral Style

The last topic in this introduction of what to assess is the combined importance of personality and behavioral style with experience and previous results. In my experiences earlier in my career working in a firm comprised only of other psychologists, a great deal of emphasis in our assessment work was placed on personality, thinking style, and leadership style. In contrast, I have seen search firms place particular emphasis on previous business results in a candidate's career. Rarely does the leadership research-based world of psychology interact with the "what have you done for me lately" world of executive search. Yet the complete list of what to assess, which therefore guides the assessment to be as thorough as possible, should include both of these worlds – behavioral style and previous results.

Pulling It All Together

In summary, what should be assessed in senior executive assessment? The challenge is to make this list or description comprehensive, well indexed and organized, non-repetitive, and as concise as possible. I have never seen a senior executive successfully address all of the factors on these types of lists fully. But the richer list leads to a more complete inquiry, and this leads to an informed discussion about the tradeoffs in a given individual. This is important because in my experience, most failures in selection and succession decisions are due to errors of omission (decision-makers after the fact exclaiming that they should have looked at a certain characteristic or they should have used a certain methodology).

Therefore, the list of items to be considered should include:

1. factors that are important across situations as well as an approach that takes into account the specifics of the situation;

2. a format that includes success and failure factors (failure factors should not repeat other content in the list by being the negative version of a success factor);
3. a format that includes both personality/behavioral style and experience/previous results.

With all of this in mind, the "Good to Know" box includes a summary or index of what should be assessed in senior executive assessment. This is a product of my experience (reading through hundreds of position specifications and hundreds of sets of competencies across industries, conducting assessment work in these contexts, conducting validation work in some of these contexts, and ascertaining the effectiveness of hiring and promotion decisions), my reading of relevant organizational research, my reading of the popular press and business publications, and the white-paper research conducted by me and my team of colleagues. This also includes many discussions with CEOs and board members on this subject.

Below I will discuss several topics that are embedded in or relate to the Senior Executive Assessment Factors.

Dual Capability

The concept of dual capability is included in four of the success factors toward the top of the list on the next page. The complexity facing senior executives leads to the need for paradox and breadth of capability in the senior executive personality. Overall, these paradoxes mostly have to do with the combined need for a senior executive to be broad, open, and proactive while also being focused, practical, and outcomes oriented. What is important is that the Senior Executive Assessment Factors seek to reconcile and integrate these different needs. I have noticed that a significant portion of individual leadership research and popular press articles tend to reveal the importance of one extreme or the other – the need for breadth versus depth, optimism versus realism, reflectiveness versus decisiveness, and results orientation versus effectiveness with people. The truth is that what is needed is the ability to operate in different parts of these continua depending on the situation.

Therefore, adaptability needs to combine with an ability to assert so that assumptions and the superfluous can be challenged. The

Good to Know:

Senior Executive Assessment Factors

I. Across most situations
   A. Personality and leadership/management style
      1. Vision, strategy, and thinking
         a. Dual capability in being able to be agile/integrative/broad in learning and thinking, as well as being able to develop a deep/"core" understanding of issues
         b. Dual capability in being able to anticipate and reflect, as well as being able to be decisive
         c. Dual capability in being able to be optimistic and realistic
      2. Ensuring tactical success
         a. Dual capability in being able to be hands off and hands on
         b. High standards for him/herself and others
         c. Active manager of performance
      3. Relationships and communication
         a. Insightful and accurate regarding others
         b. Capable of empathy and effective listening
         c. Can communicate effectively with different types of people
      4. Self-management and resilience
         a. Insightful and accurate regarding self
         b. Open to criticism
         c. High levels of endurance
      5. Motivation
         a. Interested in/motivated to be a senior executive
      6. Absence of the following failure factors:
         a. Excessive ego/self-promotion
         b. Excessive distrust and blaming
         c. Ineffective prioritization
   B. Experience/previous results
      1. Business outcomes
         a. Created and maximized success in more than one business entity
         b. Demonstrated the ability to sustain commercial value in a business entity
         c. Raised the profile of his or her business entity
         d. Overall experience leads to perceptions of credibility with the CEO, the board of directors, and investors/owners
      2. Leadership outcomes
         a. Broad groups of people respect, trust, and follow him or her; others pay attention to him or her
         b. Has hired, developed, and retained truly excellent talent
II. Fit to the situation – possesses experience or a behavioral style that can fit:
   A. Current and upcoming business stage/scope/scale
   B. Current and upcoming strategies and tactics
   C. Industry/market
   D. Functional depth and/or breadth required
   E. Organization's definition of ethical/acceptable behavior
   F. Current and aspired organizational culture
   G. Relevant geography

senior executive also needs to expect success, frequently identify potential and opportunity, take calculated risks, and never feel like a victim while also being evaluative, vigilant, and clear in identifying problems. Successful senior executives must consider multiple options ahead of time and consider ramifications of decisions and actions while knowing when to make a decision and take action. Finally, they need to know how to get work done through others by being hands off yet know when to be personally involved in issues and detail. Broadly speaking, this is the cognitive complexity and wisdom that Richard Kilburg has emphasized in his writing about executives.

Bob Kaplan, formerly of the Center for Creative Leadership and now a principal in the consulting firm Kaplan DeVries, has done some new and pioneering work in trying to measure these multiple capabilities. Kaplan DeVries has developed the Leadership Versatility Index. This questionnaire measures a senior executive's versatility on two complementary pairs of leadership dimensions: being strategic versus operational, and being forceful versus enabling. They summarize their perspective and approach in the instructions for their questionnaire:

> Each pair is a combination of opposites. To be good at both sides of oppositions or dualities like these is to be versatile. Many leaders, however, are better at one side than the other. They are lopsided. Your scores on this instrument will give you a reading on the extent to which you are versatile or lopsided.

Learning Agility

Versatility is not only about breadth in capability, it is also about being an efficient learner so that one can know how to apply one's capability depending on the situation. The first item in the Senior Executive Assessment Factors emphasizes the importance of agility and distilling the complex. Bob Eichinger and Michael Lombardo have been conducting research about the importance of learning agility for both senior executive performance as well as high-potential managers. They have observed in their research that successful leaders:

> learn faster, gaining their lessons closer to on-the-spot, not because they are more intelligent, but because they have more learning skills

and strategies that help them learn what to do when they don't know what to do. They also are more open to what they don't know. They are energized by the challenge of learning how to do something better and differently.[5]

When I have talked to successful senior executives' peers and direct reports across organizations and business situations, by far the most frequent comment I have heard from these colleagues is that the successful senior executive is a "quick study." This is learning agility.

Executive Intelligence

The Senior Executive Assessment Factors also address the recent work on different "intelligences" beyond raw cognitive ability that are important to senior executive performance. Justin Menkes has written about a broad set of thinking styles that he has bundled under the label of executive intelligence.[6] He organizes executives' intelligence into three types – thinking regarding tasks, thinking regarding other people, and thinking regarding themselves. Examples in the category of thinking regarding tasks include: anticipating obstacles and identifying sensible means to circumvent them, critically examining the accuracy of underlying assumptions, and using multiple perspectives to identify probable unintended consequences of various action plans. Examples in the category of thinking regarding people include: recognizing the underlying agendas and motivations of individuals and groups involved in a situation and anticipating the probable reactions of individuals to actions or communications. Examples in the category of thinking regarding themselves are: pursuing feedback that may reveal errors in judgments and making appropriate adjustments, and recognizing personal biases or limitations in perspective and using this understanding to improve thinking and action plans. Much of this content is in the Senior Executive Assessment Factors under Vision, Strategy, and Thinking, Relationships and Communication, and Self-Management and Resilience, respectively.

Emotional Intelligence

Some of Menkes' factors overlap with the concept of emotional intelligence (developed by John Mayer, Peter Salovey, and Daniel

Goleman). Emotional intelligence is basically the ability to read and use emotions in an effective way as one acts and responds in different situations. Emotional intelligence also has received a lot of attention lately. It has become a useful concept to which to attend in assessment because some senior executives succeed independent of high levels of intellect. The concept has been catchy because we all know of senior executives who have been very successful, yet they were not "the smartest person in the room." Goleman, along with Richard Boyatzis and Annie McKee, applied emotional intelligence to management in the book *Primal Leadership: Learning to Lead with Emotional Intelligence*.[7] They organized emotional intelligence into four categories: Self Awareness (including items such as accurate self-assessment), Self Management (including items such as self-control and optimism), Social Awareness (including items such as empathy), and Relationship Management (including items such as teamwork and collaboration).

Relationships as Opposed to Interpersonal Skills

Sessa and Taylor distinguished between relationship and interpersonal skills during a discussion on emotional intelligence in their book, *Executive Selection*.[8] Interestingly, they highlighted the difference between interpersonal savvy, which is often associated with first impressions, and the more long-term, deep interpersonal awareness and effectiveness associated with relationship skills. This distinction can be found in the Senior Executive Assessment Factors as well. Often the surface-level interpersonally based competencies are grouped together during executive assessments and related decision-making, but it is important to note their differences. Given the nature of relationship skills, they are more difficult to assess than interpersonal skills using interviews, but they are extremely important for senior executive success. I have found that they are best detected using references with peers and direct reports as well as some self-report instruments that will be discussed in more detail later.

A Cautionary Note: The Role of Charisma

I purposely have not mentioned charisma in this chapter about what to assess for several reasons. First, I believe the desired relationship, communication, and motivation style of a senior executive should be mostly about match to organizational culture as opposed to a broad ability to be socially captivating and inspirational. Second, the Senior Executive Assessment Factors list already includes the constructive components of the charismatic personality, such as vision, being able to capture others' attention, and earn others' loyalty. Third, most researchers of charisma in leadership propose that charisma can lead to excessive ego and excessive self-promotion. These are failure factors to be avoided. Fourth, I could label only about one-third of the effective senior executives with whom I have worked or whom I have assessed as charismatic. In conclusion, I am wary of decision-makers who blindly support or do not support candidates based on the elusive definition of charisma. Rakesh Khurana published an interesting book on this subject – *Searching for a Corporate Savior: The Irrational Quest for Charismatic CEOs.*[9]

Toxic Leaders

Kathy Schnure and several of her colleagues at Georgia Tech conduct research on toxic leadership and its impact at senior organizational levels. Schnure summarizes this research below. Toxic leadership is a new "buzz phrase" in the realm of executive assessment and organizational psychology. Broadly defined, toxic leaders are individuals who are characterized by destructive behaviors, dysfunctional interpersonal interactions, and a tendency to exploit or harm others for their own gain. Given the popularity of the topic, some are quick to label a demanding boss or a wheeling-and-dealing politician as "toxic," but in its purest sense, toxic leaders are those who are truly detrimental to organizations in their quest for power.

Toxic leadership can come in many forms and in varying levels. Under the "umbrella" of toxic leadership, psychologists have researched the toxicity of those with high levels of aggression, those with clinical or subclinical borderline personality disorders, sociopaths, and people with clinical and subclinical narcissistic personality disorders. Those who are on the fringe or outskirts of the "normal" population range in any of these areas could run a high risk of exhibiting behaviors associated with toxic leadership if placed in a managerial position. In the following section, I will spotlight one of those "toxic" trait areas, and discuss the good and bad associated with bringing an individual who may qualify as a clinical or subclinical narcissist into an organization.

Toxic Leadership Spotlight: Narcissism

The *Diagnostic and Statistical Manual of Mental Disorders IV* (DSM-IV), which serves as the go-to guide for defining mental health disorders, classifies those with narcissistic personality disorder as individuals who:

- are preoccupied with fantasies of unlimited success;
- believe that they are special and unique;
- require excessive admiration;
- possess a strong sense of entitlement;
- are interpersonally exploitative and lack empathy;
- exhibit high levels of arrogance.

Narcissism can extend beyond the realm of psychopathology, and can be found in varying levels among the general population in the form of subclinical narcissism. In the realm of subclinical psychology, narcissism is broadly defined by researchers as a grandiose sense of self-importance.

Some other researchers consider narcissism to be a form of "defensive self-esteem management." This defensive self-esteem management is based on an overwhelming need for approval, and can result in behaviors that look much like "delusions of grandeur," with the person truly believing that they are ultimately superior to all others, and that they are entitled to more than everyone else. Narcissists strive toward absolute perfection, which is obviously something that is impossible to obtain in practice. But, in order to continue to see themselves as being as close to "perfect" as possible, narcissists will inflate their own opinions of themselves as a defense mechanism to aid them in warding off any negative feedback that may come their way.

Narcissists thrive on praise from others, yet oddly, a common practice of narcissists is to alienate others with their lack of empathy and frequent exploitation of those in their social circles. These opposing behaviors cause a vicious cycle that causes these individuals to seek praise from others, and then subsequently alienate them. This paradox creates a situation that requires immense effort of the part of the narcissist either to regularly seek out new social connections or to take on roles at the helm of large groups.

One of the most toxic behaviors that a narcissist in a leadership role can exhibit is known as "narcissistic rage." The fragile self-images held by narcissists are easily threatened, and they often respond to any perceived threat to their self-image with "narcissistic rage," which is characterized by hostility, extreme anger, and hypersensitivity. Practically speaking, this means that even the most minor difference of opinion between a narcissist and another person can trigger an extremely hostile and over-the-top reaction that is completely unwarranted by the reality of the situation at hand. Clearly, a leader who consistently flies off the handle without reason can create an extremely toxic working environment for those around him or her.

Another potential problem with narcissists in the workplace stems from a disconnect between perceived success as a leader and the subordinate ratings of the leader. Despite the outward charisma in narcissists, their subordinates often do not find their leadership skills to be effective, while narcissists believe their leadership skills to be far superior to those of others. This disconnect can be problematic in situations that require a realistic view of one's own capabilities. Narcissists are likely to take on more than they can handle, and then pass blame to subordinates when the job can't be completed properly.

"The Productive Narcissist"

There are those that acknowledge the "productive" side of narcissism, claiming that narcissists' need for reaffirmation and admiration leads them to excel in certain areas. According to this conceptualization, those with narcissistic tendencies have a strong need to be dominant over others, and to gain authority in order to prove themselves. As a result of spending years trying to outdo others and prove themselves, it seems that narcissists often end up in leadership roles. Furthermore, personality characteristics that are typically viewed as being positive traits in leadership roles, such as extraversion, dominance, warmth, and social boldness, are often found at high levels in the personality test results of people who may later exhibit narcissistic behaviors in the workplace. Possessing these characteristics can make narcissists attractive candidates for important positions or for positions with high levels of visibility in a company.

There are two additional characteristics of "productive narcissists" that aid them in ascending to leadership roles: they tend to be visionaries, and their confident vision enables them to inspire a number of followers. Having spent much of their time charming people in order to elicit praise, they then use that same charm to encourage the masses to get behind their broad visions and ideas. Their ability to articulately describe their ideas, innovations, and visions, coupled with their apparent self-confidence and air of superiority, give narcissists the element of "charisma."

When holding leadership positions, narcissists can often inspire rapid, marked change in order to continue their never-ending quest to obtain power, praise, and glory. A narcissist's level of confidence as perceived by others can be beneficial to a group, in that the group will tend to "get behind" an idea because the group leader seems to be so sure of the idea's success. Narcissists show patterns of risk-taking that can often spur innovation, vision, and definitive action, often giving them an entrepreneurial talent.

Assessing Narcissists

It can be difficult to "diagnose" narcissism or detect narcissistic tendencies during an executive assessment. Narcissists have an uncanny ability to manage they way they present themselves to relative strangers, and work diligently to make a positive first impression. Typically, it is only as they begin to interact more frequently with a person that they begin resorting to the exploitation, manipulation, and deception that is associated with narcissism.

In a one-to-two-hour interview with a stranger, a narcissist will likely make a concerted effort to make a positive first impression on the interviewer. It is far more likely that a narcissist would display the "positive" aspects of narcissism during an interview or assessment – exhibiting extraversion and social boldness, appearing to be decisive and proactive, and directing their interviewer toward their track record of innovation, creativity, and important accomplishments – as opposed to the traits associated with the "dark side" of narcissism. In an interview or assessment setting, these would all be extremely desirable qualities in a candidate in most situations involving high-level corporate roles. The people conducting assessments are typically trained to identify potential narcissists by noting that they sometimes have too much charisma, and seem to identify themselves as corporate heroes; some can be extraordinarily talented at masking or hiding any negative characteristics they may possess.

It is important to have an understanding of how narcissists function in various situations so that their behavior can be more easily predicted, so that perhaps some of the toxic behaviors can be stopped before they begin. Perhaps most importantly, being aware of a predisposition toward narcissism can allow Human Resources professionals and high-level management to keep an eye on the person in order to ensure that if the narcissist begins to cross the line from toxic behaviors to truly toxic leadership that is detrimental to the organization.

Types of Experience/Previous Results

The business outcomes section of the Senior Executive Assessment Factors list orients the assessor toward gathering proof regarding the assessed senior executive's association with previous desired results. Making a case for reliability and consistency is why one item in the list addresses success in more than one situation and another item addresses success over time. While the "raising the profile" part included in the third item may appear like a surface-level point and sound like it lacks realization that business is usually and ultimately a team sport, this item addresses the salience of previous success. John Wilder, former Chairman and CEO of $46 billion TXU, told me once that one area he examines when evaluating a senior executive is whether an individual has led a clearly successful area of responsibility and has become known for a significant success.

The last business results item is the extent to which a senior executive possesses credibility in the eyes of the senior executive's current or prospective bosses. The identity of those bosses differs in obvious and subtle ways depending on the position and therefore should be vetted fully ahead of time. For example, a CFO's bosses are usually the CEO and the board's audit committee. A CEO's bosses are the board and perhaps several key regulatory body leaders, depending on the industry and situation. As the reader can understand, the respect-

and credibility-based relationships with these main governing entities by themselves can make or break senior executives' tenures.

The leadership outcomes section places emphasis on leadership-oriented perceptions as important areas to test. The word leadership is used intentionally here and sparingly throughout the rest of this book. For these purposes, I define leadership as displaying senior-level influence in bringing new levels and types of results to an organization. It is important that decision-makers can answer the question: Has the leadership experience that a senior executive possesses led to respect, trust, and "followership" in the eyes of the different key groups of people he or she has led previously? In other words, is there proof that the individual under consideration can win the hearts, minds, and attention of different constituencies? This is the ultimate area to probe regarding people leadership.

In addition, the second factor in this section addresses a major set of outcomes related to this respect and trust – the successful track record in building and maintaining an organization through successful hiring, development, and retention. Does the leader hire well? Does the leader pay attention to his or her own succession? Does the leader retain effective performers?

Fit

My observation has been that CEOs and boards talk more about fit than actually being thorough about it. They spend more of their time deliberating about the qualities of candidates rather than digging deeper and systematically under the surface to get at the needs of situations (which are sometimes not obvious). To be clear, when you ask them, most will believe that a CFO for one situation may not be right for another situation. But they tend to evaluate fit as they consider and respond to a real candidate or person who is active within a given assessment process, rather than getting out ahead of this fit issue. They may do this out of some sense of efficiency and because they ultimately feel "they will know the right person when they see him or her." This can happen to CEOs and boards for several reasons:

1. They become distracted by the real candidates they have "in hand" (for example, debating their tradeoffs amongst personality weaknesses and experience gaps), and spend more time analyzing the

person(s) "in front of them" than the situation that lies "in the background."

2. They can miss the opportunity to clarify what is important to fit because they can feel that fit criteria are obvious enough and permeate the entire decision process; unfortunately, fit issues often remain unspoken (and these issues therefore escape debate).

3. Aspects of fit are considered amorphous, too esoteric, or difficult to clarify by some (for example, fit to organizational culture).

4. They attend to one aspect of fit (for example, business scope and scale), but miss other aspects of fit (for example, geographical fit).

5. The Senior Executive Assessment Factors list includes seven different and important aspects of fit – some decision-makers may feel there are too many of them, such that it is difficult to analyze them in a proactive and efficient way.

6. They can be uncertain as to whether to look at fit to the current business situation or fit to business situations in the future.

7. When trying to look into the future, they can either be uncertain about how far to look or believe that future change will be too difficult to predict.

It is important to clarify several aspects about fit. First, no overall list like the Senior Executive Assessment Factors list is ever complete or perfect for every situation. This is one of the problems with "leadership recipe" books. The wording "across most situations" was chosen for the first section in the Senior Executive Assessment Factors list specifically because some of the factors in that part of the list may need added emphasis, rewording, or de-emphasis depending on the situation.

Second, this list does not ignore the importance of being clear at a granular level about the duties and responsibilities that are found in job descriptions and specifications. This is why a great deal of the assessment work I have seen conducted of an executive team comprised of different roles addresses executive team-level competencies to facilitate across-group comparisons and specific factors related to position. This last part is done by: (1) utilizing a separate competency labeled functional expertise/breadth of experience, (2) comparing candidates to specific job descriptions, relating to near-term (for example, hiring, promotion, M&A integration) versus longer-term (succession) questions, and (3) making use of the aforementioned empirical benchmarks that define a profile of competency scores that are related to success for a given position.

Fit to Scope and Scale/the Challenge of Potential

Executive recruiters tend to search for external candidates who have direct and successful experience with a given business stage (for example, CEOs who have experience commercializing a new product where the technology company is in its second major round of venture capital funding) and experience with a given scope and scale (in terms of revenue, number of employees, and diversity/difficulty of groups to be managed).

Relating to scope and scale, what if a direct size match cannot be found (or recruited) readily? What if it is a promotion or succession situation in which only internal candidates are being considered and none of them has experience that matches a need? In either case, a guess must occur about whether something in a person's career to date can predict success if a person makes a jump to greater scope and scale. This is the ultimate, core question involved in determining whether someone is "high potential" or not.

Pete Hart, former President and CEO of MasterCard, once conveyed to me that finding new ways to detect senior executive potential is more important than ever because there are fewer people who are likely to follow others these days. The point was that it is more difficult than ever trying to discern who the real leaders are, given that many people engage in leader-like behavior. In addition to generational shifts in behavior, a related point is that shifts in demographics may lead to added importance in discovering potential in mid-level managers. Ed Michaels and his colleagues at McKinsey stated as they made the case for an upcoming "War for Talent" in the foreseeable future that "the demand for bright, talented 35 to 45 year olds will increase by 25% and the supply will be going down by 15%."[10]

Ram Charan, Stephen Drotter, and James Noel[11] have developed the most useful framework I know of for thinking through size-related potential. This conceptualization is especially appropriate for understanding senior executive potential because the model substantially involves large business organizations that by definition feature a rich array of potential senior executives. The authors wrote:

The starting point is understanding the natural hierarchy of work that exists in most organizations ... In a large, decentralized business or organization, this hierarchy takes the form of six career passages or pipeline turns. The pipeline is not a straight cylinder but rather one that is bent in six places. Each of these passages represents a change in organizational position – a different level and complexity of leadership – where a significant turn has to be made.

These critical career passages are: Manage Self, Manage Others, Manage Manager, Functional Manager, Business Manager, Group Manager, and Enterprise Manager. By comparing an open position's location within this framework to a candidate's history of success and pace in traversing this framework, a more informed guess about that candidate's match to the size of the new opportunity can be made.

Organizations such as Personnel Decisions International and Development Decisions International (DDI) have each conducted research designed to separate potential from current knowledge and skills. DDI, for example, separately measures Job Challenges (what one has done), Organizational Knowledge (what one knows), potential (what one is capable of), Personal Attributes (who one is), Personal Development Orientation, Balance of Values and Results, and being a Master of Complexity. Again, the reader can identify many of these themes in the Senior Executive Assessment Factors list.

I believe senior executive assessment is different from assessment at lower levels in an organization in that there is always a potential component to senior executive assessment, even in hiring situations. I do not remember ever having a decision-maker ask me to just limit my assessment insights to the obvious components of the immediate situation. The line of questioning across all senior executive contexts is: Could this person do more? Could this person adjust if this change occurs in our market and I make that change to their responsibilities in the next quarter?

At a practical level, my view of the research about executive potential leads me to give four responses whenever I am asked what "indicators" best predict potential to take on more:

1. Has the candidate really displayed consistently good results?
2. Does a candidate frequently volunteer to take on more responsibility than what is conventionally in their role, whether this is on

a task force, committee, or true growth in responsibility? (And do they demonstrate effectiveness each time?)

3. Does a candidate frequently request feedback or comments from others in a genuine attempt to understand objectively how they are doing? (But not do so in a needy way or with everyone with whom they come into contact.)

4. Does the candidate attempt to learn what decision-making is like at the next level by frequently putting themselves in the shoes of their manager and other peers? In this way, they can privately make decisions, in parallel gain an understanding of what their boss's or peers' decision was, and then check in on the effectiveness of this decision across time. By engaging in this type of behavior, the candidate can also understand what merits attention at the next level. These candidates will frequently ask about and test their managers' decisions in one-on-one interactions.

Fit to Strategy/Tactics

Matching a CEO or senior executive candidate to a prospective company because of industry experience is frequently an automatic move for decision-makers. Yet there are several other areas of fit to consider – again, there are a total of seven in the Senior Executive Assessment Factors list. I find it useful to remind boards about one prominent example. Lou Gerstner did a great job of transforming IBM and improving the company's business performance during his tenure. Yet Gerstner had never run a technology company, let alone a computer/hardware company. The board placed a significant bet on Gerstner not because of an obvious industry fit, but because of a fit to the strategies and tactics needed in the business.

It is easy to forget how dire IBM's situation was in the early 90s. I should know. I was there – working in the U.S. business in 1991. The company lost $5 billion in 1992 – at the time a record loss for an American corporation. The Chairman of Motorola, Chairman of Apple, and former President of Hewlett-Packard all declined the CEO job in 1993. Now pretend you are on the IBM board. Even with significant players in the industry turning you down, would you have dared to go outside the industry? The board ended up picking Gerstner, who was Chairman and CEO of RJR Nabisco, a consumer products company. In addition, Gerstner previously had been at American Express.

While Gerstner's success was probably due in part to the fact that he had management exposure to the computer operations at American Express and he was informed about the market and customers' needs because American Express was a major IBM customer, his match to IBM's upcoming strategies and tactics trumped his knowledge of the industry. He had overhauled businesses, sold huge assets, and made operations more streamlined and coordinated in his career before IBM – these all were needs that IBM possessed given fast-moving changes in its market.[12] The board made the right fit-related decision by focusing on strategy and tactical needs, not (in the end) by making an automatic decision based on industry experience.

Another example regarding fit to strategy/tactics
The economic crisis of 2008 is an example of how broad economic trends have a significant impact on a senior executive's strategies and tactics. As companies retreat into a defensive, cost-saving state, the competencies needed in the senior executive levels will also shift. In this example, senior executives need to weather the storm of "recession mode," managing down-sizing, negative growth, and tumbling stock prices while helping a company come out on the other side with minimal damage.

There are few affected more directly and visibly in these crises than the Chief Financial Officer. The CFO has central responsibility for a company's bottom line, and during times of economic uncertainty there is greater pressure to provide reassurance that a company will be able to stay afloat. A flailing economy will call on a different set of skills and competencies in a CFO, and the possession of those skills and competencies may make or break not only the CFO's career, but the company itself. Though it can be difficult to predict the course of a downturn, there are certain competencies that can set a CFO apart in trying times.

Good communication is essential to almost any role, but appropriate communication to large groups during an economic downturn is crucial. The timing and content of messages delivered to both the senior team and to other employees is of the utmost importance, and those audiences are hungry for any information or words of solace. Yet in an environment filled with uncertainty, it is difficult to predict what will happen in the short term at all, let alone relay a thoughtful message regarding the state of affairs along to interested parties.

The most effective CFOs will be able to toe the line between providing open, honest information about what potentially lies ahead without either demotivating or overpromising. Someone who is an excellent listener, and who analyzes incoming information thoroughly before responding or making a decision based on that information, will be an ideal CFO during a tumultuous time.

During a time where little information about what the future holds is available, the CFO will often be charged with deciding how to cut costs. A good CFO will be contemplative, and will not jump to quick conclusions based on limited information. Will it be more advantageous to cut capital expenditures or to lay off employees? How many employees should be laid off, and how do we avoid under- or overestimating that number? Should we lay off employees consistently across all areas of the business or is there a particular area of the business that we could eliminate all together? Should we focus on certain levels or reduce headcount across all levels of the organizational pyramid? And how will these actions affect the motivation and attitudes of the human capital that remains? The effective CFO will think through all possible scenarios before arriving at a conclusion.

Jennifer Reingold in *Fortune* magazine[13] outlines more broadly how the economic crisis that started in 2008 might impact what we look for in our senior executives. She stated that a "Lifeguard" style may replace the "Lone Ranger" style. This is the case because of contextual realities such as "increased regulation, diffuse power, and stagnant stock prices." Similar to the insights about CFOs above, Reingold summarized that looking beyond the short term and inspiring employees will be important too.

Fit to Integrity and Ethics

Somewhat provocative is the inclusion of integrity and ethics in the fit section. When I am discussing what needs to be assessed in a client situation, I constantly hear that integrity and ethics are "givens" that need to be on every list. In fact, I have heard from some clients that integrity and ethics are so elementary that they do not need to be specified. Other readers also will believe that there is no relative definition of integrity or ethics depending on the situation. They believe either you have it or you do not.

My point is that integrity is always important, but that two organizations may define integrity differently. A financial trading organization will probably have a different definition of right and wrong (looser, either overtly or unwritten) than a faith-based healthcare organization (not that they are perfect in the sphere of integrity and ethics).

Fit to Organizational Culture

Organizational culture, or more frequently just culture, rolls off the lips of many people when they are talking about fit. While there are many definitions of organizational culture, the summary is that culture is the set of distinctive attitudes, values, beliefs, and "ways of doing things" that help to define and differentiate an organization. This is important because a senior executive needs to communicate and motivate using content and style that match the needs of various key constituencies involved in that organization. It can be difficult to wrap one's arms around culture because it is amorphous, but also because the issue can be confusing. Different parts of organizations can have different cultures. Some organizational psychologists also are concerned about the methods involved in measuring person–organization fit and believe that, for example, an over-emphasis on culture fit over other predictors can be deceiving. Culture can be measured through interviewing and it can be measured through surveys. I will address culture surveys later when I discuss assessment methods. The "Tips" box includes a sampling of questions that can be helpful when attempting to reveal culture consultatively.

Another important issue that arises when we are looking at the fit between a person who is assessed and an organization's culture is whether the executive should fit the current culture or a desired/aspired culture. When bringing in an external candidate to fulfill a senior executive position, especially the role of CEO, the organization is often looking to the outside because change is desired. Large-scale changes in the way things are done often coincide with a cultural shift. Therefore, the ideal candidate may not be an executive that matches

> ### Tips:
> #### A Sampling of Questions that Can Reveal Organizational Culture
>
> 1. What are the stated or written descriptions of culture and values?
> 2. In your own words, is there an aligned view about culture that applies to the entire organization? What is it? How strong is it? Are there "subcultures"?
> 3. How does the culture differ from other companies' cultures in which you have worked?
> 4. When people join the organization, what do they first notice about the culture?
> 5. What are the personalities of key leaders of the past and present? Who is a current model for the culture/who personifies the culture? How?
> 6. What are the key stories, lore, and myths from the past involving the culture?
> 7. What routines or rituals are unique or particularly important?
> 8. How do people prefer to exchange information (for example, communicate about a new initiative)? How are new ideas best introduced?
> 9. How do people socialize?
> 10. What political lessons are necessary for success?
> 11. How does the organization's compensation system work? How are people rewarded? What is rewarded?
> 12. On what basis are people hired? Promoted? Exited/fired/sacked?
> 13. In summary, when people do not fit, what tends to be the issue?
> 14. Are there any changes desired/expected in the culture?

the current culture. In these situations, I believe it is important to assess the aspired culture using a group of key individuals (e.g., board members and senior management) to define not only current culture, but the desired culture of the organization. Many assessors gloss over this important distinction.

Assessment can also be applied so that a CEO can gain a more in-depth understanding of whether a current intact team of executives, and not just one executive entering the organization from the outside, matches a culture change the CEO has in mind. The "Case Scenario" box describes a case involving assessment's role in adjusting senior executive talent to create culture change and positive results.

Case Scenario:
Culture Change

Situation: A $4 billion technology company had been spun out of a very traditional and slow-moving research organization. The CEO wanted to increase the urgency and commercial orientation in the corporate culture. He wanted to understand which of his executives would personify and help him lead culture change. The top 40 executives including the CEO were assessed. The methods were an interview, leadership and personality measures, and extensive internal referencing.

Result: Several executives' roles and responsibilities were changed based on the assessment, culminating in a larger organizational restructuring. The company's common stock price doubled in the two years after the assessment.

Summary: Determining What to Assess

Michael Frisch in the book *Individual Psychological Assessment* summarizes that most formal job analysis approaches cannot be used in individualized and unique contexts such as senior executive hiring assessment. He wrote: "the number of incumbents is often very small, openings occur one at a time, and there may be only one or two candidates for an opening. Other methods of gathering and categorizing job-related information for individual assessment have evolved – for example, asking human resource staff, hiring managers, or other subject matter experts about the key accountabilities of a job or managerial level, the knowledge, skills, and abilities required, and situational factors related to performance."[14]

1. Make a decision about how role specific you want your competencies and job specifications to be. In a hiring situation involving one position, this content describing success factors can be specific and as relevant as practical to the position in question. At the opposite side of the continuum, in many succession assessment situations, companies desire and prefer to assess a set of high-potential executives up against a set of general senior executive competencies. In this case, they are seen as members of the senior executive talent pool and a potential match to a variety of senior executive positions.

2. Place the Senior Executive Assessment Factors list in front of all decision-makers, and ask all decision-makers to provide input that will make this list specific to the situation at hand. In hiring or promotion situations especially, ensure you address five issues:

   a. What "must you have" versus "what is nice to have"? Determine this as explicitly as possible.

   b. What is important for the future that might not have been important in the recent past? How do you expect that the business will need to change?

   c. How does the successful candidate need to be different from the incumbent? Have this conversation – even if the incumbent is involved in the selection process.

   d. Consider that while external candidates may be important for certain specific business situations as discussed earlier, they also need to be noticeably better than internal candidates given their nonexistent institutional knowledge.

   e. Consider the Senior Executive Assessment Factors list within the context of the larger senior executive team. You may be able to trade off some factors in an open position if they exist in abundance in other members of a senior team. For example, Arthur Blank co-founded Home Depot with Bernie Marcus. Blank told me that as he and Marcus ran the company, Marcus was primarily the "outside-facing showman and promoter." Therefore, Blank would argue that this competency was not needed in abundance within the senior-most executive levels at Home Depot while Marcus was there. It was already covered by Marcus. See their book *Built From Scratch* for more detail on their division of labor.[15]

3. Have organization leaders respond to the questions about the organization's culture (for example, those questions contained in the box "Tips: A Sampling of Questions that Can Reveal Organizational Culture") and/or to a commercially available organizational culture survey.

Summary

The use of competencies in executive assessment allows for an objective comparison of candidates across a range of content areas. In determining what should be assessed, it is important to consider: (1) the factors that are important across situations as well as an approach that takes into account the specifics of the situation, (2) a format that includes success and failure factors, and (3) a format that includes both personality/behavioral style and experience/previous results.

There are a variety of factors relating to personality and leadership/management style that are stable across most executive assessment situations. For example, senior executives should be capable of creating vision, setting strategy, and thinking critically. They should be capable of ensuring tactical success and driving results, and they should be skilled in building and maintaining relationships and communicating effectively. Furthermore, senior executives need to be capable of accurate and honest self-appraisal and highly motivated to achieve success in their careers. In addition to these competencies, or factors, that are considered instrumental in ensuring success, there are several failure factors that are considered detrimental. Senior executives should *not* be characterized as having excessive egos or high needs for self-promotion, excessive distrust, or the inability to effectively prioritize tasks and goals. The presence of these failure factors serves as a "red flag" or warning in a senior executive assessment.

More important than simply assessing a candidate's behavioral style is answering the question of whether a candidate provides a good fit to the company, on the basis of the qualities and skills he or she possesses. That is, is the candidate well aligned with the needs and goals of the company, in terms of his or her previous experience and personal characteristics? The issue of fit is something that requires more deliberation than what I have seen typically from CEOs and boards. This chapter laid out the major types of fit to consider, including fit to scope and scale, fit to strategy/tactics, fit to industry and market, fit to integrity/ethics, fit to organizational culture, and fit to geography and physical location. These are all important aspects of fit to consider when vetting a candidate against the current and future needs and goals of a company.

Chapter 4

How to Assess

Senior executive assessments can be conducted by a variety of groups, from internal Human Resources departments to consulting firms. Each, of course, has its own set of advantages and disadvantages. While the end goal of each of these assessment professionals is reasonably the same, the assessment approach differs considerably based on the source's expertise. Yet, regardless of who conducts the assessment, it is crucial that certain requirements are met to make the process as beneficial as possible. These requirements range from the way the interview is conducted to the specific methods that should be used or combined within the assessment. This chapter will outline the common methods used in senior executive assessment and provide recommendations regarding which to use, the best combinations, and how to best deliver the assessment from setup to developmental feedback.

Virtually all senior executives have conducted interviews at some point in their career, and many of us would argue that we know the "basics" about interviewing. However, there are different types of interview methods, questions, styles, and structures that can be used in order to effectively obtain the information needed within a senior executive assessment. This chapter describes the specific methods needed to make the most of the interview time during an executive assessment. It also provides some common mistakes to avoid as well as tips on how to control the interview and obtain the best data/ information.

Another common form of assessment method is the self-report questionnaire, which is often completed online and provides information about how executives view themselves. The results of these questionnaires are often combined with other forms of assessment data. They can provide extremely valuable insights, especially when the appropriate instruments are used and effective interpretations are made. In addition to commenting on self-report questionnaires, this chapter discusses simulations, work samples, and 360 degree or multi-source approaches. My opinions and advice regarding these various types of assessment are provided. I conclude the chapter with a general outline of a senior executive assessment process and sample materials to be used (e.g., communication plan, development plan).

The Feel of Senior Executive Assessment

It is important to be rigorous and consistent in the assessment of senior executives given the importance of the positions involved, but I believe senior executive assessments should have a certain "feel":

1. Participants should not be treated in a mechanical way.
2. Nonetheless, the process should be standardized across participants in a given group and time should be used efficiently.
3. The process should engage participants and be interesting as much as possible.
4. The process should be managed by people who possess a communication style appropriate to senior executive levels.
5. The process should feel relevant to senior executive jobs.

The first important decision about senior executive assessment methods is who should conduct them in a given situation. There are several options:

1. internal Human Resources;
2. psychology-oriented firms and individual consultants;
3. Human Resources-oriented firms and consultants;
4. executive search firms.

Internal Human Resources

The advantages of internal Human Resources (HR) conducting these services is that HR professionals may have a nuanced view about what to assess given their insiders' view of the organization. Also, HR functions, especially in large organizations, may employ leadership development specialists who have expertise in executive assessment. In addition, costs can be minimized if HR conducts the work as opposed to external entities. The disadvantages are that assessment experts may not exist inside an organization's HR function – or a given organization may have experts that focus on selection at hourly and supervisory positions, but do not have experience at senior executive levels. A CEO or board may also desire an outside or independent perspective about the situation and candidates.

Psychology-Oriented Firms/Individual Consultants

The advantages of Ph.D.s and masters-level individuals in psychology are that they often have extensive experience with senior executive assessment and related tools. There are a subset of tools that should only be purchased and appropriately used by individuals trained in psychology. As mentioned earlier, the outside or independent view is often valued too. The disadvantages of using this type of consultant is that some of these individuals conducting this work may not match the senior executive presence needed for the work, they may depend too much on "canned" or "off-the-shelf" approaches, some of these groups do not have a true focus on senior executive levels, and some do not have a true international capability. An example of a large international psychology-oriented firm that conducts this type of work is RHR International.

Human Resources-Oriented Firms

Some consultancies that serve the Human Resources function (in areas such as Compensation and Benefits, Employee Communications, Outsourcing) have assessment capabilities. The advantages of this type of offering are that the work can be integrated with other activities such as executive compensation consulting, and can occur within the fabric of an existing strategic relationship. Examples of the larger firms that conduct this type of work are Hewitt, Oliver Wyman, and Towers Perrin.

Executive Search Firms

Recently, large executive search firms and smaller boutiques have started offering senior executive assessment. Search consultants in the top firms often have either line management experience in their area of specialization or business expertise that typical assessment specialists may lack. This benchmarking perspective combined with assessment data provides for a thorough assessment. The advantages of executive search firms conducting this work are that they possess many preexisting relationships with CEO and board clients, they interview at the senior level exclusively, the larger firms are truly international, and the use of search consultants within an interview can yield the benchmarking aforementioned. The disadvantages are that the methods vary greatly across firms and there may be concerns about the "poaching" of assessed internal talent (although off-limits rules apply with internal executives who have been assessed and the firms use "fire walls" to protect assessment information). Russell Reynolds Associates and Egon Zehnder are examples of search consultancies that offer a variety of senior executive assessment services.

Methods

It is best to make use of at least two types of methods when developing a senior executive assessment approach. This is because more "angles" or types of views about the behavior of a senior executive yield a more reliable or precise perspective about how that person acts or will act. The major methods options are:

1. interviews;
2. self-report questionnaires;
3. simulations and work samples;
4. 360 degree or multi-source approaches.

Interviews

This is the most common senior executive assessment method. I believe that all senior executive assessment should include an interview. Put another way, senior executive assessment should not include just self-report questionnaires or a simulation. While self-report questionnaires can be tempting in fast-moving situations, self-report questionnaires do not work well when they are the only method used and when the person and situation are complex. Within the category of interviewing, there are four types of approaches.

Para-clinical interviews
The assumption behind this approach is that there are key experiences and "under the surface" dynamics that have been involved in the development of those being assessed and are important in understanding their current and future behavior. Therefore, this type of interview might include questions about candidates' relationships with their parents so that the interviewer can understand how they interact with "authority figures." Some (but not all) senior executive interviewees bristle at these types of personal question and some may wonder about their job relevance.

A real example can be illustrative. During an interview a senior corporate development executive offered a story about his childhood to me. He was asked by his grandmother to paint the family's mailbox. As he was painting, friends came by to entice him into leaving and going swimming. He rushed the rest of the job but was stopped by his grandmother just before he was about to leave. The grandmother pointed out that he had misspelled the family's name on the mailbox. She then gave him a stern and eloquent speech about how hard members of the family had worked to make a name for the family. He was directed to fix his work and then go inside the house where he should reflect on what the grandmother had said. Based on other aspects of the assessment methodology, it was clear that this individual was distinctively focused on clarifying his accountabilities and being very intense and tireless in his follow-through and execution. One can argue that the story conveyed in the interview is useful in illustrating the work ethic of the candidate.

Situational interviews
This interview approach involves asking candidates how they would act or respond in potential or hypothetical conditions. This is appealing in that the interviewer can hear about responses to situations that the interviewee might eventually encounter in the future, given the

description of a prospective role. An example of this question would be "what would you do if you encountered a hostile line of questioning from a board member?" Some studies have found that other interview approaches, such as behavioral interviews described below, are more useful in predicting performance.

Behavioral interview s
Often paired with an extensive focus on competencies, this interview approach gained popularity at about the same time (the 80s and 90s). In this interview type, the interviewer asks the interviewee to provide an actual, relevant performance example from the interviewee's past. The assumption is that past performance is the best predictor of future performance. In contrast to the situational interview, the response to a behavioral interview question is not expected to be speculative and therefore is assumed to be more accurate. An example of this type of question would be "could you tell me about a situation in which you encountered a hostile line of questioning from a person who was senior to you?" While this approach appears to yield good levels of prediction, I have found that some effective executives are nonetheless not fluid or surprisingly uncomfortable "on their feet" in generating previous relevant episodes – their thinking does not seem to work this way. In addition, this type of questioning can be limited if one is trying to ask about a previous experience that the interviewee just does not have (for example, asking high-potential CEO candidates about their behavior in board situations when their board experience is minimal).

Many assessment professionals actively promote behavioral interviewing as the superior interview method. They contend that behavioral interviewing is the next best thing to direct observation: it pushes candidates to recall in detail what they did and said in key situations as if they were reliving them. The interview is better than direct observation in that it also allows you to review what candidates were thinking about and feeling during the situation itself. Behavioral interviewing is designed to help the interviewer obtain the kind of detail that makes it seem as if the interviewer was present at the time the previous events actually happened. It allows the interviewer to gather evidence about critical competencies in a way that is most likely to ensure that a candidate both possesses competencies and is likely to demonstrate them in situations that require them in the future.

Below are some examples of questions using the behavioral interview approach:

1. Can you tell me about a time when you contributed to the significant growth of a business or turned around a business that was failing?
2. Can you describe a time when you had to lead a significant organizational change?
3. Can you tell me about a situation where you had to overcome a significant problem or obstacle?
4. Can you tell me about a time when you had to manage people across different cultures, functions, or locations, or a time where you had to manage a diverse team?
5. Can you tell me about a time when you had to build a new organization or functional team?
6. Can you tell me about a time where you had to lead an organization through a merger or acquisition?

As follow-up to these main types of questions, the behavioral approach to interviewing often involves probing for additional information using the questions below:

1. The background to the situation
   a. What was the event about?
   b. How did the candidate first get involved?
   c. What were the key occurrences that led the candidate to feel effective?
2. The candidate's thoughts and reactions
   a. What was the candidate thinking during pivotal moments?
   b. What were the candidate's reactions at key points in the situation?
3. The candidate's behavior and words
   a. What were the candidate's key actions? What did the candidate do?
   b. What did the candidate actually say to others?

4. The outcome of the situation
   a. How did the situation turn out? What was the outcome?
   b. What would the candidate have done differently?

Chronological interviews

This interview approach has gained some momentum over the past ten years, especially in venture capital and private equity-related assessment such as with the firm ghSmart. As its name suggests, this is an intensive interview in which interviewees are asked a series of questions about business approach and outomes at each and every step of their career. For example, they might be asked about the scope and scale involved in a given position, major achievements, responsibilities enjoyed and not enjoyed, and reasons for moving to the next position. The relentless focus on detail sends a message valuing and fostering rigor to interviewees, and the recording of substantial detail aids the interviewer in identifying trends. The disadvantage of this approach is that it can be "mind-numbing," mechanical, and boring to accomplished interviewees.

"Hybrid" interview approaches

Often a single type of interview approach is preferred for a given situation, but including multiple approaches is often acceptable and encouraged. For me, the ultimate criterion for an effective senior executive interview is: Did the interview feel like a rigorous conversation in which I covered all the relevant competencies and factors? For example, behavioral style and certain leadership competencies are often assessed using a competency-based or behavioral interview format in which the executive is asked to recount prior experiences or behaviors. This format is effective in assessing personality and competencies, but used in isolation may lead to a narrow perspective of the executive's career and previous patterns of behavior. Therefore, the inclusion of a chronological account of the executive's career at the beginning of the interview, in addition to the behavioral interview questions, is necessary to understand the executive's track record and experience as well as previous behavioral trends. This is particularly common when interviews are used in combination with other assessment techniques that have highlighted certain areas for concern or

---

Tips:
Basic Interview Format

1. Review the interviewee's work history using a version of the chrono-logical approach:
   a. scale of responsibilities and people management;
   b. achievements;
   c. likes and dislikes in the position;
   d. transition rationale.
2. Use the behavioral approach to address specific competencies and factors. These should be followed by probing questions that allow the interviewer to better understand what happened.
3. Closing the interview: last questions.

---

uncertainty. In my experience, the basic format for an effective interview across many situations is shown in the "Tips" box.

Interviewing best practices
Lost in the discussion above about interview process is the importance of interviewers being observant. Besides the questions that are asked and the verbal content of responses, interviewers should attend to other factors such as tone, nonverbal cues, and even the office environment (when conducting an interview in the interviewee's office). How does the interviewee treat the interviewer? What has the interviewee chosen *not* to say? For example, I am often concerned when I have asked a series of questions about people leadership and management and an interviewee never uses the names of his or her direct reports when relating a story. What choices has the interviewee made about how his or her office is decorated?

When conducting interviews it is easy for the interviewer to make mistakes, such as moving too quickly or losing control of the interview. Using a basic interview format like the one mentioned in the "Tips" box helps protect against some of these mistakes. The creative and insightful consultants at Cambria Consulting have categorized these main mistakes and the type of interviewees involved. Many readers will recognize the types of people in this list:

- The Storyteller
  a. Provides the interviewer a great deal of context but few details.
  b. Relates the story from a third-party perspective – like a voice-over narration.
  c. Tells the interviewer about everyone else's role except his or her own.

- The Fast Talker
  a. Needs just one question to start and finish a story.
  b. Sees questions as opportunities to speak rather than to respond.
  c. Needs to be interrupted before he or she stops talking.
  d. Loves interviews, meetings, task forces, parties, etc.

- The Big Picture Person
  a. Talks in terms of grand concepts or philosophies.
  b. Sees issues from a historical point of view.
  c. Looks for opportunities to put things "in perspective."
  d. Resists behavioral detail.

- The Introvert
  a. Has difficulty in believing that you are really interested in what he or she has to say.
  b. Responds to questions with overly concise answers.
  c. Never volunteers information unless you ask for it.
  d. Takes a lot of time before responding to questions.

- The Egalitarian Populist
  a. Always uses "we"; never uses "I."
  b. Is offended that you want him or her to personalize answers.
  c. Likes to describe group efforts.
  d. Is sincere and "authentic" to a fault.

The goal is for the interview to be structured and planned, but not mechanical. In industrial and organizational psychology, there is considerable discussion about the use of structured versus unstructured interviews. Industrial and organizational psychologists widely agree that structured interviews yield higher validity and more predictive accuracy for job performance than unstructured interviews, especially when these interviews are behaviorally focused. Structured interviews are designed so that all interviewees are asked the same set of questions and scored using a predetermined rating scale. A good rating scale should consist of actual examples of behaviors that indicate a certain level of performance. Behaviorally anchored rating scales (BARS) increase reliability and add some objectivity to the rating process. These scales are often used by assessment providers, and an example for the competency of Collaboration is provided in Figure 4.1.

Other types of interview questions
I often save a few questions for the last part of the interview. In the "Tips" box above, this part of the interview was labeled "Closing the interview: last questions." The interviewee is often most open and

Definition: Builds constructive partnerships internally and externally; and encourages the active participation of others in discussions.

Excellent	5	• Leads constructive debate • Uses relationship networks strategically to accomplish objectives • Makes valuable contributions to group discussions • Clearly fosters/encourages others to make significant contributions
Strong	4	
Sufficient	3	• Maintains a network of effective relationships across the organization • Participates in constructive debate • Appropriately involves others and builds consensus • Appropriately manages conflict when it arises • Is willing to help others and share resources
Area for development	2	
Significant area for development	1	• Creates unnecessary conflict in group discussions • Avoids conflict • Does not listen effectively • Prefers to work alone and not interact with others • Does not share credit with others • Pushes his or her agenda forward without considering its impact on other areas of the organization

Figure 4.1 BARS for Collaboration

Example:
BARS

Earlier we talked about common interviewing errors. The use of standardized rating scales, such as BARS, helps prevent assessment providers from making common rating errors. Examples of typical rating mistakes are: being too lenient, being too severe or tough, central tendency errors (that is, rating everyone in the middle of the rating range on all competencies), and halo errors. Halo errors occur when the rater provides similar ratings across all competencies because one characteristic or trait is most salient in his or her mind (for example, the interviewee is rude and disrespectful), and this characteristic or trait influences all the ratings. Interviewers also bring their personal biases to interviews. For example, I see some interviewers who are more favorable to interviewees who are from the interviewer's hometown. Awareness of these rating errors and biases as well as the use of BARS helps promote accuracy.

---

disclosing at the end of the interview. Therefore, most of these last questions tend to be direct. I have attempted to group these questions into different types:

- Overall Self-Report Questions
  1. "What is your most favorite job you have ever had? Least favorite? Why?"
  2. "What work environment/culture is optimal for your satisfaction and performance?"
  3. "What types of people work best with you? What types of people do not match you?"
  4. "What do you prefer in a manager (or oversight from a board)? Who was your favorite manager? Least favorite? Why?"

- Differentiation Questions
  1. "What differentiates you from others in similar positions/how are you unique?"
  2. "How would you summarize your contributions to your organization? What achievement makes you proudest?"
  3. "What would not have happened at your last job if you were not in your role?"
  4. "What is the 'headline' on your career to date/few words or phrases?"

- Role Models/Mental Models Questions
  1. "What leaders do you look up to? Why? Compare/contrast your-self to these people and other key individuals in your career."
  2. "What have you learned from mentors?"

- Others' Perceptions Questions
  1. "What will references say about you? Your reputation? Your legacy?"
  2. "What have your bosses/peers/direct reports said about you?"
  3. "Have you ever gone through an assessment? If so, what was said about your strengths and areas for development?"

- Management Style Questions
  1. "What are the core definers of your approach to management and leadership?"
  2. "Describe your approach to project management."
  3. "Describe an example of how you have approached performance problems in others."
  4. "Tell me about a situation in which you had to 'jump start' your team's motivation after a setback."
  5. "Describe your approach to leading meetings."
  6. "Describe your approach to hiring."
  7. "Describe your involvement and success in the development of others' skills/careers."
  8. "What has been your most significant learning as a leader/manager?"

- Business Acumen Questions
  1. "What are the three main drivers related to success in your current business?"
  2. "What is an opportunity your business is not capitalizing on?

- Imminent Action Questions
  1. "What would be your first set of actions in your new job *or* what are your next, upcoming tactics/plans for your team in this upcoming quarter?"

- Motivation and Ambition Questions
  1. "What are your career objectives? Ideal job?"
  2. "What drives you?"

- Hiring/Selection/Promotion to Open Position Questions
  1. "How do you feel about the location of this opportunity?"
  2. "What are the reasons for leaving current position/reasons for being interested in opportunity?"

3. "What will be the biggest challenge in the open position?"
4. "What are your concerns about the current opportunity?"
5. "What will you do if you are not selected for the open position?"

- Final Questions
  1. "What blind spots have you come to know in yourself?"
  2. "Aggressiveness plays out in some way in all of us. How does your aggressiveness play out?"
  3. "If I were to work with you on a day-to-day basis for a year, what emotions would I see?"
  4. "What is the most common misconception people have about you?"
  5. "Is there anything else I should know?"

Self-Report Questionnaires

Self-report inventories or questionnaires consist of written questions that are completed by the assessee. While some of the options I describe in the section below may not be described always as self-report questionnaires by assessment professionals, using the above definition for this section should suffice. The assumption is that useful assessment insights can be gained by asking a senior executive candidate a series of (usually multiple choice) questions about their personality, thinking, and behavior. While there are many types of questionnaires, I will simplify the options into four main initial types to help demystify this professional area. I will then expand this section to include other options. Many of these other options represent new and exciting developments in the area of executive measurement. As you might guess, the areas of focus represented by the self-report questionnaires can be mapped onto much of the content found in the Senior Executive Assessment Factors list.

Leadership style/behavioral style
Decision-makers tend to use a common language when discussing and describing senior executives. CEOs and boards debate about how hands-on or strategic candidates are, for example. Self-report questionnaires contain questions that can help an assessment provider specify how pervasive or substantial these traits or dimensions are in a given candidate. Examples of these traits or dimensions are:

assertiveness, empathy, reflectiveness, perfectionism, listening, independence, persuasiveness, outgoingness, innovation, optimism, excitability, and boldness. These measures have grown in their use since the mid 1990s, although there is still active debate in the field of organizational psychology about their usefulness. These measures usually take between twenty minutes and one hour each to complete. They are often untimed and often can be administered securely and remotely over the Internet. The publishers of each measure should be contacted for guidance about the education and training needed in individuals who can purchase and interpret these tools. Examples of these established measures include the California Personality Inventory, NEO PI-R, 16PF, and the Occupational Personality Questionnaire-32 (OPQ-32).

The potential to "fake" or "distort" responses to personality tests or self-report questionnaires administered in senior executive assessment has received considerable research attention. The concern is that those who are in a selection situation have a great deal at stake when taking the measures involved in an assessment battery, and that as a result, they may skew their answers in a direction that causes them to appear more favorable or desirable in the eyes of those administering the assessment. This phenomenon led to the creation of "Social Desirability" scales, more commonly called "lie" scales, which are used to determine the extent to which a test-taker may be distorting his or her answers in a more culturally favorable direction.

The issue of faking has called the validity of personality measures into question, though at this juncture there seems to be little consensus over whether or not validity is ultimately affected. Some researchers believe that faking causes personality measures to be less effective, while others contend that in spite of some faking patterns on some measures the results of the test itself are not ultimately affected.

The summary of my experience is that while there is probably more faking in selection situations than pure development assessment situations, for example, I find that the faking I do see in self-report questionnaires still tells me a great deal about the assessee. This is because we all do not "fake good" in the same way. Even when candidates feel they know what the ideal candidate should look like in a selection situation, they still emphasize behaviors and traits that reflect who they are. For example, one candidate in a situation calling for a turnaround may emphasize interpersonal aggressiveness while another candidate may emphasize the importance of schedules and timelines.

Derailers
As mentioned earlier in this book, the direct and overt measurement of negative personality factors has increased in popularity amongst assessment providers. The assumption is that the conventional leadership style and personality measures are not useful enough in detecting the presence of problems with ego, relationships, and problematic approaches to decisions. So, for example, a personality measure on its own might convey that a senior executive is a 9 on a 10-point scale in assertiveness (which may appear desirable for many situations and not a problem). However, a derailer measure administered to that same senior executive might show very high emotionality or excitability. This might indicate that this individual may be direct, but that there is too much emotional volatility that accompanies the directness. A main example of a derailer measure is the Hogan Development Survey.

Motivation
Personality researchers look at the area of motivation as being different from personality. While personality is about behavioral style across time and situations, my summary is that motivation is about: (1) what drives and energizes a person, and (2) how much drive and energy a person possesses overall, especially for use in attaining objectives and overcoming difficulty. Regarding motivation definition 1, for some people, material reward is a key motivator. For others, it is learning or helping others. Regarding motivation definition 2, a fully capable personality that matches a set of senior executive specifications may or may not match the motivation level needed for a job. For example, a CEO who has taken two companies public in five years, has been financially successful, has not seen his or her family frequently, and is toward the end of his or her career may be a good competency match to a new opportunity but her motivation profile may not match the new scenario. Examples of motivation questionnaires include the Motivation Questionnaire distributed by Saville and Holdsworth (SHL) and the Motives, Values, Preferences, and Interests Questionnaire distributed by Hogan Assessment Systems.

Organizational culture

Another set of tools that are increasing in popularity are organizational culture measures. Many of these measures are in essence surveys that focus on "how things are done" at a particular organization. Each survey consists of various factors of culture such as the degree of collaboration or the amount of flexibility given to employees. Popular culture surveys are Denison's Organizational Culture Survey (DOCS) and Human Synergistics' Organizational Culture Inventory (OCI). On the downside, it has been my experience that many of the existing culture surveys are not comprehensive enough, and often fail to capture the true essence of an organization's culture (for example, is there a true interest in debating the issues in meetings and communications?).

It is my belief that the assessment of organizational culture is extremely important to the health of an organization. Organizational culture measures help ensure the well-being of a company in the following ways. First, the results bridge gaps between leadership's view of the culture and everyone else's view of the culture. When gaps between leadership and the broader employee base are found, Human Resources and Talent Management professionals can work with leaders to educate them about perceptual gaps or help reform the broader culture.

Also, these measures serve as a tool when undergoing a conscious change in culture. The current and desired states can be assessed and clear areas are identified for a company to focus on in order to achieve the desired culture state. In addition, organizational culture measures allow for more seamless integrations of different cultures in situations such as mergers and acquisitions. Discrepancies between two different organizational cultures can be identified. This aids in the proactive clarification of potential problems post integration. Also, it allows leaders from both organizations to express their desired vision in order to create a commonly agreed-upon culture. Finally, culture measures can inform the selection of senior executives who embody either the existing or desired culture. This assessment of candidate fit will be discussed in more detail later.

In order to obtain these benefits, the organizational culture survey has to measure important factors that shape and define the culture. While there is considerable consistency across surveys, each survey has its own set of factors. Some of the most common tend to be

teamwork/collaboration, emphasis on performance, flexibility, innovation, and strategic direction. The titles used to describe these factors
may vary, but these concepts are often captured in the assessment of
culture. As an example, Figure 4.2 shows the overall factors used in
Russell Reynolds Associates' culture meanure to assess organizational
culture. It should be noted that each of these broad factors has
subcategories that are included to provide more specific and detailed
information.

While organizational culture measures are typically used to
conduct an assessment at the organizational level, they can also be
helpful in doing an assessment of an executive's fit to a certain organizational culture. As was discussed earlier, approximately 50% of the
executives brought into an organization fail, and often the reasons for
this are attributed to a lack of culture fit. Therefore, the culture
measures may soon include a version in which candidates fill out a
questionnaire about their preferred organizational culture. Their
preferences are compared to the baseline findings from an organization regarding the current and/or desired culture. Degree of fit could
then be determined.

Virtually all of the CEOs and boards with whom I have worked
believe strongly in the importance of a senior executive candidate's
fit to a culture. Actually using specific culture surveys to measure a
candidate's culture fit is surprisingly new. Organizational researchers
are closing in on useful measurement in this area. Figure 4.3 shows a
sample from the Russell Regular Associates culture fit approach.

After the initial research on organizational culture or candidate fit
is done, it is often necessary to dive a bit deeper to better understand
gaps between the current and desired state, lack of candidate fit,
extreme scores, and so on. This can be done in a few different ways.
First, many of the surveys include item-level data that allows the
company or organizational psychologists to gather more information
about factor scores. There may be certain items driving factor scores
down or up. Recognizing the extreme items helps clarify the issues
that need to be addressed. For example, a progressive organization
may score moderate to low on an Innovation scale and be confused
by the result. By taking a look at the items they may find that there
is a specific issue, for example a lack of reward for innovation, that
is impacting the finding. While they may not need to change the way

Culture Strength	This index measures the strength of the organizational culture. That is, the extent to which individuals within the organization feel that there is a "culture" or set of core values that drive behavior, and the degree to which employees perceive a shared vision and feel able to articulate the general culture of the organization.
Discipline	The notion of discipline captures elements of the organizational culture relating to the rigor involved in day-to-day functioning, including the emphasis placed on ethical behavior, adherence to rules and policies, arriving on time for appointments/meetings, attending to detail, mentoring/training employees, and maintaining appropriate diligence about the organization.
Openness	An organizational culture can be defined by its openness to people, thoughts, ideas, and alternative methods. Specifically, this factor captures receptiveness to employees with unique personalities and from diverse/multicultural backgrounds, as well as elements relating to alternative work schedules and matrix-oriented organizational structures.
Strategic Growth Orientation	The extent to which an organization is oriented toward strategic growth is an important aspect of the overall culture. Organizations with high scores on this factor will place a premium on innovation, encourage long-term thinking and planning, value the understanding of customers/clients, prioritize top-line growth, value intelligence/critical thinking skills in employees, and be oriented toward global expansion.
Performance Orientation	Organizational cultures with a performance orientation place emphasis on results and high levels of performance. Specifically, this factor assesses the degree to which expertise is valued, and long working hours and hard work are expected. This factor also captures expectations about completing work quickly while maintaining a high degree of accuracy and quality.
Relationships	The norms regarding the relationships among employees and managers are an important piece of organizational culture. For example, the extent to which employees motivate and encourage each other, value a high level of personal communication, discourage interpersonal aggression, emphasize teamwork and collaboration, and develop friendships that extend outside of the work relationship.

Figure 4.2 Culture Analyst™ Factors

Respondent's Name _____John Smith_____

	Low Fit	Medium Fit	High Fit
Overall Fit to Current Culture		▓▓▓	
1. Discipline	▓▓▓		
2. Openness		▓▓▓	
3. Strategic Growth Orientation			▓▓▓
4. Relationships		▓▓▓	
5. Performance Orientation			▓▓▓

Figure 4.3 Sample from the Culture Analyst™ Culture Fit Index

they are hiring or their approach to the market, they may need to change their compensation system.

In addition to gathering more information about the item-level survey results, a consultative interview approach (also mentioned in Chapter 3) can be used to better understand an organization's culture. When applying this method, I recommend interviewing 10–15 senior executives and using a fairly structured format with specific questions about culture. I have a list of about 10 questions that I tailor to organizational needs. An example of a typical question is, "How does the company differ from its competition/other similar companies? How does the company differ from other companies in which you have worked?" Using this more time-consuming and resource-intensive process is worthwhile when a thorough evaluation of the culture is desired. Interviews help explain why certain results were found in an organizational culture survey, and what can be done to change the current norms, values, and beliefs.

Cognitive ability
It may be desirable to measure the intellect or cognitive skills of a senior executive. Most people assume at the least a broad association between intellect and senior executive performance. Research has also shown that a general relationship between intellect and performance does exist. Cognitive ability measures may address quantitative rea-

soning, reasoning when dealing with language, critical thinking, or abstract thinking, for example. I have found that most senior executive assessment professionals have their own point of view regarding which of these areas should be measured and which measures are most reliable, valid, and useful. Cognitive measures are common in some global regions (for example, the United Kingdom) but not in other countries or regions. Some senior executives respond negatively when asked to take a measure that calls their level of intellect into question. Many of these measures are timed and most must be administered or proctored in person. Two example measures are the Watson Glaser Critical Thinking Appraisal and the Raven's Progressive Matrices. The former addresses critical thinking effectiveness while the latter measures components of abstract reasoning.

One other aspect of using cognitive measures deserves mention. Written assessment reports will contain a summary of the person's cognitive performance if cognitive measures are used. This summary can be in the form of percentiles based on relevant norms or in the form of standardized category names (for example, above average) that represent certain percentile ranges. I encourage the use of the standardized category names that represent percentile ranges. Therefore decision-makers will not be able to try and interpret small and insignificant differences between percentile scores.

In addition, across time, I have found that decision-makers become attracted to this one cognitive section of the report, to the point they ignore other parts of the report. Therefore, the use of cognitive measures can result in a narrow, unidimensional consideration of the person who has been assessed. This can be limiting and misleading. I have seen this addressed by burying this section in the middle of the report so that decision-makers are forced to work through the other content.

Recent developments in cognitive measurement
There have been two developments that have led to innovative new choices in the area of measuring senior executive thinking and knowledge.

1. Situational judgment Situational judgment tests measure a person's decision-making effectiveness in key situations involved in a given position. Therefore, these tests are developed for a given position or group of positions. The test developers collect examples of typical business challenges that a senior executive incumbent will face. The assessee is then presented with these representative though directionally ambiguous situations, and must determine how he or she would address the issues presented. These responses are then scored based on an objective, empirically derived scoring scheme. The result is a situation-specific and practical measure of senior executive judgment. Besides being generally useful as a measurement approach, it appears that these measures may result in less adverse impact against minority participants than many other standardized cognitive tests. Many consulting psychologists who work with organizations have the capability to develop these measures for different assessment situations.

2. Industry-specific business decision-making Lia DiBello and a group of her research colleagues at an organization called WTRI have been developing an approach to measuring senior-level business decision-making in a very realistic manner. Decision-making is evaluated through the objective scoring of predictions made and actions indicated in response to blinded but actual case descriptions and financial data in a given industry. In other words, decisions are evaluated based on real outcomes that previously occurred in the blinded organization featured. In summary, respondents "analyze actual business situations and make actual business decisions." The format is intensive and thorough. The measure is presently available in the industries of durable goods, electronics, enterprise IT, biotechnology, and pharmaceuticals. WTRI expects to continue developing this measure for use with other industries.

Interpretation
Self-report questionnaires are most valuable when used in combination with other self-report questionnaires and when they are used in combination with other types of assessment methods. Used together, themes and interpretations about a given executive can be created by trained assessment experts. The interpretation will often identify areas for probing in the assessment interview. In some situations there are inconsistencies in the data or salient areas for concern which would have not been uncovered without the use of multiple self-report questionnaires. This is why I often advocate completing self-report questionnaires ahead of the assessment interview. Self-report

questionnaires are great for getting an overall "feel" for an individual and identifying areas to probe in an interview, but I do not believe they should be used to conduct assessments of senior executives without other assessment methods.

It has been my experience that personality measures, such as the examples given above, can often have nonlinear relationships in the way they relate to senior-level effectiveness. That is, having high levels of a certain trait (for example, extraversion) is not necessarily more desirable than having low levels. Being moderate to moderately high on extraversion is probably more appropriate and useful for many senior executive situations.

This idea contradicts the approach to typical personality research. If you were to peruse the relevant journals within the field of psychology, you would find many articles examining the linear relationships between certain personality variables (e.g., conscientiousness) and criteria such as job performance. Although this approach is often appropriate when one is dealing with selecting large numbers of candidates and there is a need for "off-the-shelf" approaches, within the area of executive assessment I advocate a focus on critical parts of a scale's ranges.

In addition to critical ranges, the interactions among scales are often extremely important for understanding the behavioral style of an individual. For example, scoring high on a scale that measures independence may be beneficial in that the senior executive will often develop his or her own perspective and be less likely to follow others blindly. Yet, when this score is combined with very low scores on scales that measure soliciting others' opinions and empathy, it may point to areas for concern. For example, this interaction may indicate that the senior executive infrequently collaborates with others and/or has an overly directive style.

Explicit steps in the interpretation of these types of questionnaires are rarely found in books and articles about assessment. Understandably, emphasis has been placed historically on the importance of experience and having an effective supervisor when learning how to make sense of these questionnaires. Given the frequency of use in using personality and behavioral style measures when dealing with senior executives, and the danger of "getting lost in the data," I think it is useful to lay out the following principles when interpreting these types of self-report measures:

1. Identify patterns/trends/themes/profiles/interactions, especially across extreme scale scores.
2. Develop a clear and concise point of view about a person's "essence" based on these identified patterns. Balance induction (considering the information collected across the entire assessment process) and deduction (using previous and relevant assessment experience and expertise) as the interpreter hones these points of view.
3. Write organization-specific and competency-specific strengths and weaknesses based on these patterns and essence. Realize that these patterns and essence are often most useful in driving the interpretation across competencies or different sections of the assessment report.
4. If the interpreter feels the need to describe someone in conflicting terms, address situations that lead to one behavior versus another. Reconcile the conflict. One of my, and my clients', pet peeves about assessment feedback and reports is when assessors are inconsistent and "talk out of both sides of their mouths."

Simulations and Work Samples

One trend found in the previously mentioned innovations in cognitive ability measurement is that the measures are practical and have a strong resemblance to the types of decisions and situations that a senior executive might actually face. Simulations and work samples are other approaches involving realistic previews of senior executive situations.

Homework

Periodically I have observed CEOs who will spontaneously spring upon external candidates what I call a "homework assignment" during the selection process. Usually it involves giving candidates time to think through the implications of a new strategic direction or to recommend improvements to a business unit. The candidates must in short order (3 days, for example) articulate and defend their point of view with the decision-maker. The advantage of this approach is that it gives the decision-maker a clear understanding of how those assessed will make decisions and act in a real situation impacting the organization. The disadvantage is that homework requires that the decision-maker reveals detailed (and potentially sensitive) information about the organization to candidates who, if external, may not end up joining the organization.

The four remaining simulations and work samples are classic "assessment center" components – that is, they are standardized simulations that are administered to a group of candidates and scored. Some senior executives find them contrived, "junior level" in feel, and uncomfortable. Others find them relevant and interesting, especially those whose jobs and experiences possess an orientation toward science.

Case analysis and presentation

Case analysis occupies the space in between the substantial length and objectivity of the industry-specific, questionnaire-delivered, case-oriented decision-making measure developed by WTRI and the subjective nature of the homework assignment. In the typical case analysis and presentation example, the assessment provider either obtains a commercially available (and usually general and industry agnostic) business case, or develops one for a specific assessment context. The senior executive being assessed reviews the case and then usually within an hour or so must present his or her analysis and recommended actions. The assessment provider then uses an objective scoring scheme to evaluate the assessee.

Inbox exercise

During inbox or in-basket exercises, assessees are presented with simulated correspondence, memoranda, calendar items, and other documents. Assessees must prioritize the areas to which they will attend and respond accordingly during a given timeframe. As with the case analysis and presentation, general versions of inbox exercises are commercially available or they can be custom developed for a given situation. As you would expect, many inbox exercises are now administered electronically and can include real-time changes and complications.

Leaderless discussions

This is a group activity, therefore it is used when multiple individuals are being assessed at one time and in one location (this is frequently not the case in senior executive situations, and certainly not in hiring contexts). In leaderless discussions, a handful of assessees are given a problem to solve. All of them are to play the part of equals without clearly defined roles. The group of individuals deliberates in a conference room. The presence and absence of leader-like or "leader emergent" behavior is recorded by trained observers. Again, the directions for conducting these activities are commercially available or they can be developed for specific situations.

Role plays

In role plays, someone plays the role of a character in a semi-structured way and presents the assessee with a realistic job situation. Example job situations include performance counseling or a meeting with a customer. Personnel Decisions International includes press interviews/conferences and meetings with investor analysts in their CEO-related assessment processes. The assessee interacts with and responds to the actor. During the role play, an observer counts key behaviors and evaluates the effectiveness of the assessee through the use of objective scoring.

The above methods primarily involves the individuals being assessed. The final category of methods below can only be applied when the involvement of others outside of those being assessed is acceptable. It is challenging to use these multi-source approaches in especially sensitive and confidential situations. Multi-source methods are best applied when there is a strong developmental component to the assessment work as well.

360 Degree or Multi-Source Approaches

This approach involves the collection of other people's perceptions about the assessee. These perceptions can be collected via hardcopy written surveys, electronic written surveys, or interviews in person or over the phone. Regardless of method of delivery, this type of approach keeps the identity of the provider of perceptions confidential (although periodically I come across organizations that experience problems with distrust about confidentiality of hardcopy or online 360 degree surveys). This method was created as a development-oriented tool in which data and reporting were only provided to the assessee. More recently, multi-source approaches have been used in evaluative or decision-making contexts in which decision-makers may view related summary data and reports as well.

The advantage of the survey approach within this multi-source category is that it is efficient and a large number of ratings can be collected. A large number of ratings improves the reliability of measurement. The main challenge with hardcopy or online 360 degree surveys is that if a rater is providing input about five or even ten colleagues, that rater has a lot of "paperwork" to complete. The advantage of the multi-source interview approach is that while some ratings can still be collected verbally, there is opportunity to collect more information via the tone of comments made about the assessee, and to engage in reactive probing based on initial responses to standardized questions. Because I believe that one can gain richer information about an assessee via the multi-source interview approach, I generally recommend it in most senior executive assessment situations. The multi-source interview approach is also useful when assessing competencies such as relationship skills, where the subtle nuances regarding an executive's interpersonal awareness and depth of relationships are better detected through conversations with those that know him or her well. This approach also is more likely to yield anonymous verbatim quotes that are compelling when included as a part of the assessment report. This format makes it difficult for those assessed to rationalize or discount difficult feedback.

To facilitate reliability and confidentiality amongst multi-source approaches in senior-level assessment, I recommend that at least three peers and three direct reports take part in a given process for an assessee. In this way, if the data reported is broken down by category (one rating average is from peers' ratings, another rating average is from direct reports' ratings), the assessee will still experience difficulty if he or she wanted to identify how individuals rated him or her. It is also important to ensure that no names or identifying information is used from this part of the assessment process so that multi-source participants can be as candid as possible and so that assessees have no opportunity to retaliate against colleagues who provide negative feedback.

In senior executive assessment, the manager of the assessee is often the CEO client for the assessment work. These CEO clients may or may not want to participate in the multi-source process. When they do not, it is usually because they want an independent view of their direct report in the assessment that is not influenced by their own opinion.

In determining who is contacted to provide their perceptions via survey or interview, I usually ask that the assessee submit an initial list. The individuals who will provide their perceptions should be informed about the assessee and are or have been a key stakeholder in that person's performance. I then ask that this list be reviewed by the manager of the assessee and a relevant Human Resources professional to ensure that it does not primarily consist of references who will only share a positive view of the assessee.

A typical format for standard multi-source interviewing is found in the box "Tips: Basic Multi-Source Interview Format." On a related note, obtaining negative information in multi-source interviewing can be difficult. The box "Tips: Probing for Negative Information during Multi-Source Interviewing" includes tips and questions that can yield important negative information about an assessee.

Special Section: Getting to the Core of Integrity

Integrity is a notoriously difficult area to measure in senior executive assessment. When clients ask me how integrity can be most accurately understood in an assessee, I invariably respond that multi-source referencing (internal and/or external) is the best approach. In those assessment situations in which I have had behavioral confirmation of low levels of integrity, the references describing these low-integrity individuals have used terms such as: "I have seen different levels of integrity in Bob depending on the situation," "he is not always open and direct," "his agenda is not always clear," "he tends to change his story as he pursues his objectives," and "his short-term view of results can lead him to act in an 'end justifies the means' kind of way." I especially am convinced of a person's high integrity when positive integrity-related referencing comments are voiced at the beginning of a reference's overall list of attributes about the assessee (such that there is no prompting about the subject matter – integrity). They have used words such as: "principled," "a stand-up person," and "straight as an arrow." While some assessment providers may use integrity questionnaires, I have not found them to be frequently used for senior executives. Many of these existing integrity questionnaires are more "junior" in their focus and attend to items such as stealing staplers and other office products.

Tips:
Basic Multi-Source Interview Format

1. Introduction.
2. Describe purpose of the project (for example, succession management or development).
3. Explain confidentiality.
4. Ask reference in what capacity they know the assessee.
5. Ask for the assessee's key overall strengths and contributions to the organization.
6. Ask about overall areas for development.
7. Have the reference rate the executive being assessed using the set of competencies identified for the project (for example, Vision and Strategy, Relationships, and Leadership).
8. Ask for examples that illustrate these ratings.
9. Ask for concluding comments.

Tips:
Probing for Negative Information during Multi-Source Interviewing

1. Have the assessee contact the reference giver to appeal for thoroughness and the inclusion of "areas for development."
2. Emphasize confidentiality at the beginning of the referencing conversation.
3. Mention that "no one is perfect" before asking for areas for development.
4. Ask "in what areas does he or she need to learn the most to help him or her be successful?
5. Ask "what advice would you give to his or her boss/prospective boss?"
6. Ask "what business situations would not match this person?"
7. Ask "when he or she makes mistakes, what do the mistakes tend to be about?"
8. Ask "what would this person's worst critics say about him or her?"

A few years ago I also worked with Robert Hogan and his team at Hogan Assessment Systems to try to identify some of the core issues at work in low-integrity executives. This work was previously presented at the 2003 Society for Industrial and Organizational Psychology Conference as well as in *BusinessWeek*. The idea was that many who work with and amongst executives have come across stories like this: A general ledger Finance executive had a long tenure with his organization. He had a low-key personality, melded "into the woodwork" and was not "flashy." Then it was discovered subsequently that this executive used his knowledge of the financial processes at the company to take extremely large payments out of the company's accounts whenever he felt he was due a salary increase or bonus. The feeling was, "the heck with it," "I am going to get my fair share."

A lot of the thinking about integrity-related problems in executives has focused on constructs like Psychopathy, Aberrant Self-Promoters, and Narcissism (for example, the Narcissism components such as the outward display of arrogance). Yet, the people I know who have worked with John Rigas, who was CEO at Adelphia, and Dennis Kozlowski, who led Tyco, have told me that neither person fit the behavior patterns that many commonly associate with executive wrongdoing. When I looked at the Industrial and Organizational Psychology research literature addressing integrity and dysfunctional behavior in leaders, there were subtle clues that integrity is related to detachment and aloofness.

Clinical psychologists and psychiatrists base their diagnoses on a handbook called the DSM-IV. I believe a component of DSM-IV's narcissism definition does a good job explaining problems with integrity, and this construct is entitlement. Remember the Financial executive I mentioned earlier who paid himself large, unapproved amounts of money when he felt he deserved it? More than anything, he was sneaky. I believe this sneakiness, based on feelings of deservedness, is more directly related to executive integrity problems than overt arrogance. DSM-IV defines the entitlement portion of narcissism as "unreasonably expecting favorable treatment, or an automatic granting of one's own wishes."

The Hogan Development Survey (HDS) uses some of the taxonomy from DSM-IV. I thought it would be interesting to develop two profiles via the HDS that might be related to different parts of narcissism, and see how they do up against a real group of low-integrity people. One profile represented a person who communicates well and smoothly, is haughty and pompous, and is brash and "shoots from the hip." The second profile (the entitlement profile) represented a person who is aloof, guarded, indifferent to others, and possesses hidden resentment toward people.

Since low integrity can be defined as breaking laws and rules, we looked at the extent to which these two profiles existed in a sample of felony inmates at a maximum security prison. Admittedly, this sample is comprised of people who were convicted of breaking many types of laws, not specific to business or executives. Nonetheless, it is a sample that explicitly addresses law-breaking in the real world.

Here were the results: The entitlement profile was present to a far greater extent than the haughty profile in this law-breaking sample. Sixty percent of the prison group possessed the entitlement profile. On average, the prison group scored over the 85th percentile on two of the defining factors of the entitlement profile. In comparison, the prison group scored on average around the 43rd percentile on the haughty profile.

We also addressed another burning question: How prevalent are integrity problems in executives? How bad is it? For example, when I asked friends, associates, and clients what percentage of executives they feel possess low integrity, I have heard everything from 1% to a friend on Wall Street who said 50%. Kevin Murphy, a prominent organizational researcher, estimated a base or usual rate of nontrivial theft in organizations at 5%. As another point of comparison, approximately 3% of adults in the United States are either behind bars, on probation, or on parole, according to the Justice Department.

We found that the percentage of Fortune 200 executives (overall sample of 1,416) who possess the entitlement profile was 13%. Based on this HDS measure of entitlement, one out of eight executives can be termed high risk for low integrity.

There are over forty published integrity questionnaires and tests, and 15–20 are in widespread use, according to Murphy. However, it is my opinion that there are few measures of integrity that are particularly useful and appropriate for senior executives. When I asked three of the active researchers in this area, none said a good measure of executive integrity exists. The HDS is a good measure in general and may be useful in attending to integrity, based on further research. Conceptually, entitlement appears to be useful in driving to the core of executive integrity problems.

In terms of practice, the American Psychological Association's position on integrity tests makes a lot of sense. Overall, personality measures like the HDS that are used to understand behavioral styles related to integrity should be treated the same way personality measures are treated in a conventional executive assessment. No cutoff scores should be used. In the integrity context, the HDS should be interpreted by a psychologist who integrates this data with data from several other personality measures. The assessment process addressing integrity should include questions and probes. Bringing us full circle, this is why multi-source referencing is important to integrity measurement.

Finally, here is an example of how a recent entitlement profile manifested itself in the real world. I will give you the highlights of the notes from two interviewers who interviewed an executive who scored as possessing the entitlement profile. They knew nothing of this research or this executive's personality data. "Seems dishonest. Hides information. Portrays himself as someone he is not. Allowed money to be loaned out from the company's trust. Bad temper. Conniving. Uses smoke screens."

How to Determine What Assessment Methods to Use

There are a handful of factors that must be weighed together when determining how to assess senior executives in a given situation. Below is an outline to provide guidance regarding the major decisions:

1. The job specifications, requirements, and set of competencies influence methods. In one context in which strategic and visionary thinking are important, cognitive measures and personality measures involving innovation should be chosen. In another context in which community relationships are important, interviews, multi-source interviewing, and personality measures involving relationship skills would be useful.
2. Determine what the duration of time should be for the total set of methods. The realistic range of options starts at two to three hours on the low end and stretches to two days on the high end.
3. Ensure representation of the major methodologies. For example, choose an interview, multi-source referencing, several personality measures, a cognitive measure, and one simulation or work sample. Again, the more angles or types of observation about a person, the more reliable the assessment will be.

4. Take into account organizational culture when choosing methods. A distrusting and private culture may result in a more abbreviated methodology. I also recently worked with a large bank that possessed a very deliberate culture. The result was that the CEO desired a longer (four hours) interview than my frequently used length (three hours).
5. Take into account an organization's history with assessment methods. An organization may have had a bad experience, for example, with the over-emphasis of cognitive scores or with confidentiality breaches with 360 degree surveys. The assessment professional either needs to reeducate the organization about the constructive nature of the previous methods or omit this type of methodology.
6. An external assessment consultancy may be able to make use of internal or corporate resources. One common way this plays out is that many organizations administer a 360 degree or multi-source survey periodically. I have seen some situations in which this data is used in conjunction with other data collected by an external assessment consultancy. Also, the assessment consultancy may partner more actively with internal HR or Talent Management professionals. For example, I am currently working on a program with Motorola in which I am conducting assessment interviews alongside Motorola HR and Talent Management professionals. These same Motorola colleagues are also conducting some of the multi-source referencing phone calls. This sharing of the methodology can result in decreased costs and increased knowledge transfer about the methodology to internal assessment providers. There is no doubt that in the future these Motorola colleagues will conduct more of the methodology themselves.

The Steps in Setting Up a Senior Executive Assessment

1. Clarify the purpose(s) of the assessment and who will be assessed.
2. Determine who will conduct the assessment and in what timeframe.
3. Determine which decision-makers will receive the verbal debrief/presentation and written report(s), and determine how and when those assessed will be debriefed about their own assessments.

Those assessed are usually provided their feedback after the debrief with decision-makers so that the feedback can be informed by the point of view of the decision-makers. Also, clarify the length of time that the assessment reports should be considered valid.

4. Finalize what will be assessed. This usually includes a senior executive-level set of competencies but may also include job specifications/descriptions.

5. Finalize assessment methods. Because of the international nature of senior executive positions, this should include a clarification as to what language(s) will be most appropriate for interviews, questionnaire material, and reports.

6. Effectively communicate about the assessment to those who will take part:

   a. In many selection/hiring assessments, this may take the form of a phone call from the hiring manager, a Human Resources professional, and/or assessment provider.

   b. In more multifaceted succession or talent review projects, this may take the form of emailed memoranda from and/or in-person discussions with the CEO and introductory meetings with assessment providers.

   c. Keep in mind that memoranda should go not only to those who are being assessed but also to those who will provide their perceptions in 360 degree and multi-source surveys and referencing.

A sample Communications Plan for a Succession Management/Team Review project is shown in the Example box (in this material, the word participant refers to the person being assessed).

Dealing with participants' concerns
To best address any concerns in those who will be assessed, I encourage Communications Plan content that includes the following points: (1) the use of assessment methods is now common; (2) these methods do not take the place of your past performance and results; (3) these methods do not take the place of your relationships within the organization; (4) the process is multifaceted – if you feel that you did not show your best within one component of the methods, you have the opportunity to represent yourself during other components. Especially in the case of hiring assessment, I emphasize that the process focuses on degree of fit. This is mutually beneficial – neither the

Example:
Executive Assessment Project Communications Plan

1. _____ to have an introductory discussion with each participant by (date) (see Talking Points below).
2. _____ to send an introductory email to each participant by (date) (see Email Content for Participants below).
3. _____ to send an introductory email to each person providing references by (date) (see Email Content for Individuals Taking Part in the Multi-Source Interviews below).

Talking Points for _____
1. One of my key responsibilities is to ensure the ongoing development and sustained high quality of leadership capabilities at _____. Effectively addressing this responsibility impacts the success of the organization in both the near and long term.
2. An Executive Assessment project is the front-end component to a broader process in which I want to make sure we focus on leadership development and succession management.
3. Substantive Executive Assessment consultancies can be helpful resources in this regard. I would like to utilize the services of _____ to conduct an Executive Assessment project at _____. They can distinctively offer unbiased and benchmarked input about leadership development and succession. This is a straightforward project comprised of four main steps.
4. First, on _____ you will be emailed guidance about how to complete online leadership and management questionnaires. This gives you the opportunity to describe your leadership, management, and work style. Along with this email containing the online leadership questionnaires, you will be asked to email a resume or summary of your career. The purpose of this resume is to help the interviewers understand your background as they prepare for the interview.
5. Second, a three-hour interview meeting in/at _____ will be conducted on _____ with two consultants to discuss your career activities, responsibilities, and achievements. One of these consultants is _____ and the other is _____. Their biographies are attached to this document.
6. Third, _____ will conduct multi-source referencing phone calls during the dates of _____ of your direct reports and _____ of your peers. The objective is to gain colleagues' perceptions of you so the assessment team can learn what it is like to work with you. _____ will contact you to ask whom you would like to serve as your references. Please choose individuals who can be informed, thorough, and willing to include areas where you can develop. _____ will review this list.
7. Fourth, once they have prepared their insights, the assessment team will make presentations to _____, and then to you. _____, and most likely the board's Governance and Nomination Committee, will see summary information so that they can generally understand the leadership capabilities of the organization. The assessment team will subsequently schedule a meeting with you to discuss their insights. You will be able to keep your personal detailed report that will be useful for leadership development.

Email Content for Participants
One of my key responsibilities is to ensure the ongoing development and sustained high quality of leadership capabilities at _____. Effectively addressing this responsibility impacts the success of the organization in both the near and long term.

An Executive Assessment project is the front-end component to a broader process in which I want to make sure we focus on leadership development and succession management. Executive Assessment consultancies can be helpful resources in this regard. I would like to utilize the services of _____ to conduct an Executive Assessment project at _____. They can distinctively offer unbiased and benchmarked input about leadership development.

This is a straightforward project comprised of four main steps:

1) On _____ you will be emailed guidance about how to complete online leadership and management questionnaires. This gives you the opportunity to describe your leadership, management, and work style. Along with this email containing the online leadership questionnaires, you will be asked to email a resume. The purpose of this resume is to help the interviewers understand your background as they prepare for the interview.
2) A three-hour interview meeting in/at _____ will be conducted on _____ with two consultants to discuss your career activities, responsibilities, and achievements. One of these consultants is _____, and the other is _____. Their biographies are attached to this email.
3) _____ will conduct referencing phone calls during the dates of _____ with _____ of your direct reports and _____ of your peers. The objective is to gain colleagues' perceptions of you so the assessment team can learn what it is like to work with you. _____ will contact you to ask whom you would like to serve as your references. Please choose individuals who can be informed, thorough, and willing to include areas where you can develop. _____ will review this list.
4) Once they have prepared their insights, the assessment team will make presentations to _____, and then to you. _____, and most likely the board's Governance and Nomination Committee, will see summary information so that we can generally understand the leadership capabilities of the organization. The assessment team will subsequently schedule a meeting with you to discuss their insights. You will be able to keep your personal detailed report that will be useful for leadership development.

Email Content for Individuals Taking Part in the Multi-Source Interviews
One of my key responsibilities is to ensure the ongoing development and sustained high quality of leadership capabilities at _____. To help our senior leaders develop and to enhance our ability to achieve desired business results now and in the future, _____ has retained _____ to undertake a Leadership Assessment for a small group of our leaders. Besides Interviews and Online Leadership Questionnaires involving the executive being assessed, the project involves a 30-minute on-the-phone multi-source interview meeting in which you are asked to communicate your perceptions about one of the leaders being assessed.

You have been chosen because of your ability to offer an informed, thorough, and balanced view of the person being assessed. We ask that you express yourself with as much directness and clarity as possible, while attending to a focus on helping each leader improve and develop.

The source of multi-source interview comments (your name) will not be reported to the individual being assessed. The assessment team is looking for reliable themes across those individuals giving references. The multi-source interview themes are integrated with trends in the interviews and other leadership questionnaires mentioned above.

I understand that you are busy, but I need to convey that this project is important and a priority. Please be as responsive as possible when _____ contacts you.

| **Tips:** |
| **Should the CEO be Assessed in Projects Involving that CEO's Team?** |
| CEOs can send a powerful signal to others in the organization if they take part in assessment projects, such as talent reviews. Taking part lets others know the project is important and worth others' time. The involvement of the CEOs often serves to decrease the anxiety levels of others. The modeling involved in this action is itself effective leadership. To maximize impact, I encourage CEOs to be the first to be assessed in a given project. As with all assessment, who will receive the deliverables must be clearly delineated ahead of time (i.e., do members of the board receive any reports or debriefing about the CEO?). In my experience, CEOs take part in about 40% of the relevant projects. |

candidate nor the organization will be satisfied if there is not a substantial fit between the candidate and the organization.

7. Coordinate and administer assessment methods.
   a. Sometimes this involves the assessment provider developing customized methods, sometimes this involves the purchase of commercially available methods.
   b. Senior executive scheduling is an art form. Make use of administrative professionals who are organized, take initiative, and are assertive. The authority implicit in the use of CEOs' assistants can lead to increased responsiveness and efficient scheduling as well.
   c. Conduct update meetings or phone calls when conducting large projects.
   d. Because many leadership-style self-report measures may be sent electronically to those who are being assessed, ensure spam filters/blockers do not inhibit the receipt of these measures.
8. The assessment professional then integrates data and information from all sources and writes the reports.
9. Conduct debrief presentation with decision-makers and feedback sessions with those who have been assessed.
10. Some assessment providers do not give assessment feedback to external candidates who are not hired. Whenever possible, some form of feedback should be given to unsuccessful external

candidates. Michael Frisch suggested in the book *Individual Psychological Assessment* that: "written reports, however, are often viewed as the property of the sponsoring organization, especially if they are customized to a specific competency model, and so are not usually provided."[1]

11. When applicable, conduct a separate subsequent development planning session.

   a. This development planning session is different from the initial assessment feedback session.

   b. At the least, these development planning sessions involve the assessee and his or her manager. The development planning sessions sometimes involve a representative from Human Resources and the assessment provider.

   c. The goal in this session is: (1) to prioritize areas for development, (2) be creative in thinking through steps in development, and (3) be practical in leading to an implementable and verifiable plan.

   d. These plans need not be long and can include different categories: (1) new behaviors, (2) education and training courses, (3) coaching, (4) books, and (5) DVDs. I have found it helpful to initially prepare a menu of options. Because every individual learns in a different way, the menu helps facilitate the more specific match between an individual's development need and his or her learning style. This is part of what is discussed during the development planning session. A concise sample development plan is shown in Figure 4.4.

12. Link the assessment to ongoing, internal Human Resources and Talent Management efforts. I also have found that some organizations integrate the components from the assessment process (for example, competency frameworks) into their own performance management systems.

13. Most assessment professionals consider that assessment results are valid for three years. This information should be included in the report itself. If a decision is to be made about an individual who was assessed more than three years earlier, the individual should be assessed again. Most assessment professionals also consider the retention of assessment material for seven years to be best practice.

GOAL	ACTIVITY	TARGET DATE	RESOURCE
1. Ensure more consistent follow-through with direct reports	– Develop a report detailing the assigned responsibilities and deadlines for the upgrade of the MGT mutual funds and variable annuities/life sub-accounts software.	July 1	Mary Steele, Assistant
	– Verbally review the status of activities in the above report during every bi-weekly staff conference call.	Bi-weekly after July 1	
	– Follow up via a one-on-one phone call with each assigned individual whose activity contribution is late.	Bi-weekly after July 1	
2. Drive continuous improvement in product development processes	– Ask team to identify procedures that could be streamlined in the Partnership Workstation project.	July 15	Michael Jennings, Director
	– Reevaluate each of the four integrated modules in the Partnership Workstation project.	July 30	
	– Reevaluate the interface with the multiple portfolio accounting vendors in the Partnership Workstation project.	August 15	Susan Brand, (external), ITM
3. Deepen investment knowledge within team.	– Identify members of team who do not hold Series 24, 7, and 63 Securities Licenses.	July 15	Sara Evans, Director
	– Select three of these individuals to commence process to gain their Licenses.	July 30	Sara Evans, Director
	– Work with HR to identify NICSA-related activities for the continued learning of the team.	August 15	Peter Franklin, Director, HR
	– Ensure quarterly learning seminars are conducted.	Quarterly after August 15	

Figure 4.4 A concise sample development plan

Summary

While the methods and approaches in senior executive assessment differ depending on who is conducting the assessment and the type of project, there are certain requirements necessary for truly effective assessment. For example, the best executive assessments include an interview with a candidate to better understand his or her experiences and work style. I have discussed many assessment options (e.g., simulations, self-report questionnaires), but having an assessment interview is core to the process. While the use of an interview may sound obvious, there is no question that the oncoming march of technological advancement will make it tempting for many assessment providers (and client organizations) to use non-interview products and methods even at senior executive levels.

Given that the style of interviews may differ, I have outlined certain best practices in this chapter that should be used by senior executive assessment professionals, ranging from the interviewer's demeanor to the types of questions to ask. One of the most common interview types used in senior executive assessment is a behavioral interview, in which executives are asked about their past experiences. While behavioral interviewing gleans important information and is well respected in the field of Industrial and Organizational Psychology, I recommend combining approaches in a "hybrid" interview in which situational, general, and other questions are asked too. The interview should contain questions about the executive's career history including key achievements and likes/dislikes, behavioral questions, and concluding questions that allow the interviewer to better understand the executive.

Interviews are often combined with other methodologies such as self-report questionnaires, simulations, work samples and 360 degree or multi-source approaches. While many of these can provide helpful information about the executive's work style, abilities, skills, motivations, and potential derailers, they need to be used appropriately in order to be effective. For example, the utility of self-report questionnaires is highly dependent on skilled interpretation. Simple rules of thumb (e.g., more of a trait is better) often do not work. Using the principles for interpretation that I outlined in the chapter, self-report questionnaires can be an extremely valuable tool. Similarly, multi-source interviews (360 degree referencing) provide depth and further support for assessments made during the interview, but are most effective when the appropriate people are chosen to conduct these multi-source interviews and when they are structured around core competencies.

While I will not repeat the details outlined in this chapter regarding how best to set up an assessment, what the process should look like, and which methods to use, I do want to emphasize a few crucial best practices associated with successful senior executive assessments. First, there should be a thorough plan in place prior to beginning the assessment process. This plan needs to begin with thoughtful consideration of why the assessment is needed and how it will be used. Second, the way the process is communicated to the senior executive assessed is extremely important. All communications (e.g., emails, meetings, and the introduction to the process during the interview) send a strong message and will impact a candidate's comfort and engagement. Finally, I have described various forms of assessment and listed many of the common instruments, but the way in which these instruments are used and combined significantly impacts their usefulness.

Chapter 5

Additional Practical Decisions

Now that the "what" and the "how" of senior executive assessment have been described, this last chapter conveys added information and guidance about related areas. As discussed previously, senior executive assessment is a core set of processes. Because there is tremendous breadth in application, there are a host of topics related to actually conducting the work. This chapter contains the practical lessons learned about these myriad topics. I believe they are especially useful because many of these items catch an organization that is new to senior executive assessment "off guard."

Senior executive assessment is (and should be) frequently tied to facilitating the development of the person being assessed. Among other content, I will lay out what CEOs and Human Resources executives have told me is most important when choosing an executive coach. Executive coaches have become ubiquitous. This chapter provides guidance on how an organization can best use them.

Earlier there was discussion about the type of "tone" that is most useful in senior executive assessment interviews. This discussion is extended to a treatment of how assessment professionals can best work with CEOs and boards. Additional guidance is also provided about how to set the right tone for communications that go out to an organization about an assessment. Leaders of organizations frequently and understandably want to know how to best introduce the concept of assessment.

An important set of decisions accompany every assessment project in terms of what reporting format should be used, and how data should be used and stored. Specific report formats will be shown and the main universe of report components will be discussed. What norms and benchmarking data are available is also conveyed so that right comparisons can be used in a given assessment project. I also will discuss data privacy and the increasing complexity involved in conducting assessments on a global scale. Finally, I will extrapolate and project out where I believe senior executive assessment is headed in the future.

The major alternatives and recommendations about the core methods involved in senior executive assessment were addressed in the previous chapter. This chapter describes other practical issues and decisions that must be considered when pulling together a successful senior executive assessment process.

Development Revisited

A large banking client of mine had a history of not emphasizing development at the senior-most levels of the organization. Sound familiar? As we conducted a succession- and development-oriented project with this bank, I had conversations with the CEO about his role in the follow-up process. The bells went off in his head when he likened ongoing development goals in his senior executive team to "non-financial objectives." He had followed up diligently for two decades about executives' "financial objectives" in a consistent and disciplined way. He learned to use his follow-up approach for these development objectives too. This group of senior executives has been very focused on their development since this project concluded. The CEO meets with them twice a year to discuss progress on (and update if necessary) the non-financial objectives. In summary, there has been much that has been written about CEOs spending a significant amount of time being Chief Talent Officers – this is one practical example of how it can play out.

In addition, Marshall Goldsmith is an active consultant and coach with senior executives. He has conducted some useful research that sheds light on the importance of this type of follow-up. He found that when executives' managers "did not respond or follow up" regarding executives' development efforts, only 18% showed top-level improvement in leadership effectiveness. When executives' managers "did respond and engage in consistent periodic follow up, 86% showed top level improvement in leadership effectiveness." My team finds similar results when we administer follow-up 360 degree or multi-source surveys after an initial assessment project has taken place and after a development plan has been instituted.

Coaching

One of the most common development recommendations after an assessment has been conducted is to provide a senior executive with a coach. While the decision is common, it was my observation that organizations were not all that systematic or informed as they sought coaching resources. Further, most of the books and articles about coaching tend to be written by coaches. Four years ago I thought it would be useful to ask CEOs and leaders in Human Resources who were experienced in purchasing coaching services a series of questions. I thought their answers would be of practical use to others who might end up in their shoes. The results of this survey are below.

Method of Survey

- Phone survey conducted with 22 respondents.
- Industries represented: Real Estate, Forest Products, Manufacturing, Professional Services, Financial Services, Telecommunications, Pharmaceutical/Healthcare, Oil/Gas, Retail/Consumer, Technology.
- Number of total employees in respondents' organizations ranged from 100 to 140,000.
- Revenue of respondents' organizations ranged from $30 million to $38 billion.

Mentoring

Before focusing on coaching, I asked the related question:

1. Does your organization have a formal executive mentoring program?
   Yes   47%
   No   53%

Internal Coaching

Before focusing on coaching primarily provided by external resources, I asked:

2. Does your organization offer formal coaching through internal resources?

Yes	36%
No	50%
Under development	14%

Organizational Levels

3. At what levels do your coaches commonly work?

Above VP	13%
VP and above	25%
Director and above	37%
Manager and above	25%

Reasons for Coaching

4. What is the reason for pursuing coaching?

Help high potentials	42%
General improvement	42%
Fixing/turnaround	16%

Number of People Being Coached

5. How many people are in active coaching relationships now?

Organizations up to $499 million	8.2
Organizations $500 million to $4.9 billion	41.8
Organizations above $5 billion	63.3

Hiring a Coach

6. Who makes the final decision to hire a particular coach?

HR professional	43%
Line management	24%
Coaching participant	33%

7. Who pays for coaching?
   HR   39%
   Line management   61%
8. What is the typical format for pricing?
   Per hour/per day   54%
   Project   46%
9. Do coaching projects have a timeframe or are they open-ended?
   Timeframe   59%
   Open-ended   41%
10. Are your coaches independent practitioners or part of a firm?
    Independent   56%
    Firm   44%
    • When asked, most indicated "no preference."
11. Overall, what criteria tend to be used in the selection of coaches?
    Coaching experience/track record
    Business experience/orientation
    Interpersonal style/"chemistry"
    Listening skills
    "Thought out" process/methodology
    Directness/candor
    Insight into human behavior
    Influence/persuasiveness
    Flexibility

Managing the Coaching Process

12. What is the typical duration of coaching relationships?
    10.9 months
13. What is the ideal duration of a coaching relationship?
    7.5 months
14. What is the actual frequency of contact?
    Every 2.4 weeks
    • Most desired more frequent contact at the beginning of the coaching relationship.
15. What is the usual type of coaching contact?
    Phone   36.4%
    In-person   63.6%

16. Do your coaches use written development plans?
    Yes   63%
    Sometimes   26%
    No   11%
17. Is "homework" a part of coaching process?
    Yes   78%
    Sometimes   11%
    No   11%
18. What characterizes activity in a coaching session?
    Conversation   88%
    Learning activities   12%
19. To what extent are participants linked to other learning resources?
    High   8%
    Medium   50%
    Low   42%
20. Are you given status reports about developmental progress?
    Yes   28%
    Yes, at a broad level   50%
    No   22%
21. Does coaching content remain confidential or is it shared with some members of the organization?
    Confidential   56%
    Broad issues are discussed   44%
22. Does coaching serve as an information gathering tool for upper-level managers?
    Yes   50%
    No   50%
23. How do you measure the effectiveness of coaching work?
    Observe outcomes vis-à-vis plans   40%
    Nothing   23%
    Follow-up survey   20%
    360 degree survey   10%
    ROI analysis   7%

General Coaching Benchmarking

24. Is coaching better than group training given a standard topic?
    Yes   81%
    No   19%

- Several respondents doubted, however, that coaching was more cost effective.

25. What development need is most frequently addressed by coaching in your organization?

Use of influence	19%
Communication skills	16%
Emotional maturity/stress management	13%
Building teams	13%
Building relationships	13%
Teamwork with peers	10%
Listening/empathy	10%
Developing direct reports	6%

26. Should coaches go through independent certification?

Yes	56%
No	44%

27. What is the degree of personal content (discussion about outside of work issues) in coaching sessions?
    23.8%

28. Do you provide coaching for leaders who have just joined your organization?

Yes	40%
No	60%

- Respondents expressed substantial interest.

29. Overall coaching satisfaction rating:

Very satisfied	34%
Somewhat satisfied	31%
Neutral	27%
Somewhat dissatisfied	4%
Very dissatisfied	4%

30. What factors relate to the most substantial coaching results?
    Personal motivation level of participant
    Management/organizational support and involvement
    Motivation to keep job or gain promotion
    Partnership/chemistry between coach and participant

31. What will your demand for coaching be in the next 12 months?

Increase	44%
Stay the same	44%
Decrease	12%

Other Practical Issues

There are a host of issues and decisions to consider when conducting senior executive assessment. Attending to these proactively can make a big difference in the level of effectiveness in a senior executive assessment program or project.

1. CEOs and boards as clients

CEOs and boards represent a unique client segment. They are busy, they are experienced, and they think quickly, broadly, and deeply. Therefore, in order for assessment work to have desired impact, several items should be taken into account:

a. Think proactively about what the board needs.
b. Involve key members of the board in scoping the project and determining competencies/position descriptions, especially when the project involves the assessment of CEO and CFO candidates. This often means interviewing separate non-executive Chairmen, lead directors, and the directors who lead relevant board committees (Nomination and Governance, Compensation, and Audit).
c. Lead the board through decisions during project design or introduction. Also communicate a point of view about methods and approaches. Be willing and able to articulate and defend this point of view.
d. Couch methods, presentations, and reports in terms of the business model, strategy, and imminent tactics.
e. Be clear, be practical, be logical, and be concise. Do not communicate much detail or research unless the CEO or a board member shows an interest in this. As leadership consultant Bob Kaplan conveyed, it is useful to communicate the simplicity in conclusions that are the result of an understanding of complexity and the fuller set of options. Do not feel the need to describe the full complexity or "boil the ocean."
f. Corporate boards and large groups of senior-level decision-makers are notorious for disagreeing and meandering in their decision process. Assessment providers need to confront boards about the specific areas of disagreement or areas that are unclear.

They should actively facilitate alignment of expectations and priorities.

g. It has been my experience that every organization, CEO, and board differs such that the identity of who presents assessment conclusions and in what format varies greatly. For example, in senior succession management situations, I have seen the CEO, the leader of Human Resources, or one to two members of the external consulting team present the material solely or in various combinations. These presentations are sometimes made to a board committee (such as Nominating and Governance), while other times they are made to the full board. I have also seen the board receive the full set of materials including complete reports about individual senior executives and I have seen them receive summaries. I have seen situations in which the board has been asked to return the hardcopy material after they have reviewed it or been allowed to retain it. The important point is to be planful, proactive, and clear from the beginning of the project about these items.

2. Communication to participants

When assessment projects and programs go wrong, a main reason is that there is inadequate communication to the people being assessed (or to the multi-source respondents who will be providing their perceptions about a person being assessed). In senior executive assessment, I strongly recommend that this communication be personal in nature. This communication best comes from the senior-most executive decision-maker and sponsor of the work and in many cases, the assessment provider. In-person communication is best. I often recommend using a hardcopy or emailed memorandum in parallel such that the purpose, methods, and deliverables are made clear and can be reviewed subsequently if there is a question. Examples were included earlier. If the assessment provider is a part of an external consultancy, I recommend that a biography of the project manager be included in this material as well.

3. Norms and benchmarking

For a client who is reviewing assessment information, it can be natural to want an understanding of how the person assessed compares and contrasts to groups of interest (this involves norms) and to effective groups of interest (this is benchmarking). The most common norming approach is data-based or empirical in nature. For example, an assessed executive's scale score from a self-report leadership measure (such as boldness) can be compared and contrasted to a United Kingdom boldness norm that the test distributor can provide. In addition, many organizations and assessment consultancies maintain their own norm databases for these comparison purposes. Below I will first describe database-oriented norming in more detail. Then I will describe subject-matter-based benchmarking ratings and the use of these ratings in databases.

Table 5.1 displays an example in which an executive team's average competency scores are compared and contrasted to a norm group (based on a proprietary database) comprised of: all other companies in the database across sectors, other industrial companies in the data-

Table 5.1 Comparison of competency ratings to database

	Integrity	Stewardship	Business Acumen	Organization Development	Teamwork / Collaboration	Global Perspective	Innovation	Commitment to Excellence	Average
ABC Company	4.4	4.0	3.9	3.1	2.9	3.2	3.3	3.9	3.6
All Other Companies	3.7	2.9	3.3	3.0	3.1	2.7	3.2	3.5	2.8
Industrial Companies	3.5	2.8	3.0	3.0	3.1	3.0	3.2	3.2	2.8
Consumer Companies	3.6	2.7	3.2	3.0	2.9	2.8	3.1	3.4	2.8

Rating Scale:
1: Significant Area for Development
2: Area for Development
3: Sufficient
4: Good
5: Excellent

base, and other consumer companies in the database. In this case, the client can review how his or her team stacks up against the competency averages found in other sectors/industries. In Table 5.2, the same type of contrast analysis can be conducted for self-report leadership questionnaire data. In this case, the CEO client wanted to compare and contrast his ABC company to both industrial and consumer companies because he was trying to move the company's traditional industrial orientation to a company that looked and acted more like a consumer company.

Somewhat more rare is effective data for benchmarking purposes. Part of this challenge is: (1) finding senior executives who have been truly effective (or clearly ineffective), (2) identifying which of these individuals have been substantively successful because of their individual characteristics – and not contextual factors (such as favorable market conditions) or chance, and (3) collecting their assessment-related data.

A new approach to benchmarking involves the use of subject matter experts. A CEO or board member can gain an understanding of how a candidate compares to the other talent in an industry or function if the person assessed is interviewed by an expert about the relevant

Table 5.2 Comparison of questionnaire data to database

	Persuasiveness (1–10)	Modesty (1–10)	Reservedness (1–10)	Vigor (1–10)
ABC company	3.7	7.0	7.1	7.9
All other companies	4.9	3.9	3.3	6.3
Industrial companies	4.8	3.2	3.0	6.1
Consumer companies	6.1	3.1	3.2	6.5

Interpretation:
• This group of executives scores as less persuasive, more modest, and more reserved than the comparison groups of executives.
• This group, however, scores as more poised for action than the comparison groups given the relatively high vigor average.

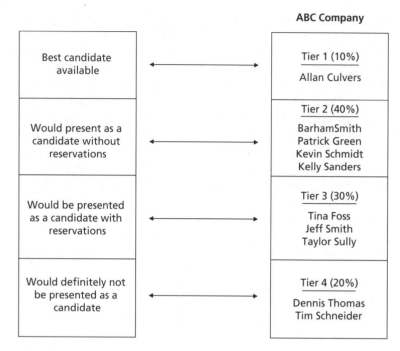

ABC Company

| Best candidate available | ←→ | Tier 1 (10%) |
| | | Allan Culvers |

Would present as a candidate without reservations	←→	Tier 2 (40%)
		BarhamSmith
		Patrick Green
		Kevin Schmidt
		Kelly Sanders

Would be presented as a candidate with reservations	←→	Tier 3 (30%)
		Tina Foss
		Jeff Smith
		Taylor Sully

Would definitely not be presented as a candidate	←→	Tier 4 (20%)
		Dennis Thomas
		Tim Schneider

Figure 5.1 Individual executive benchmarking

	Benchmarking Ratings Average
ABC Company	3.47
All other companies	2.84
Industrial companies	2.84
Consumer companies	2.89

Benchmarking Rating Scale:

4: Best candidate available
3: Would present as a candidate without reservations
2: Would be presented as a candidate with reservations
1: Would definitely not be presented as a candidate

Figure 5.2 Executive team benchmarking

talent in that industry or function. A CFO expert can then describe in words and ratings how a person assessed compares to the general group of CFOs, or CFOs in a particular geography or industry.

One type of subject matter expert that can be useful in senior executive assessment contexts is specialized, senior-level search consultants. Many of them have significant line management experience or functional management experience in their chosen areas of specialization. They possess an extensive network of relationships in that industry or function. They are interviewing and conducting references about talent in that industry/function every week, and they are involved in practical deliberations about position fit every week. Therefore, a search consultant can offer their industry/functional point of view about an assessed person – this can be useful in presentations and reports to decision-makers, and in the feedback meeting and reports involving the person assessed. A CEO and board member can understand in a practical way whether the assessed talent "is as good as it gets" or whether the organization can do better in a given position.

An example of a typical chart depicting this type of benchmarking rating for an executive team is provided in Figure 5.1. Figure 5.2 provides sector/industry comparison and contrast information similar to what is depicted in Tables 5.1 and 5.2. In this case, the CEO client can understand in summary how a talent expert would benchmark his or her team to their current respective responsibilities, and how this average benchmarking rating compares to the benchmarking averages in other sectors/industries.

4. Typical Components of the Senior Executive Assessment Report

Assessment reports' content will vary based on the purpose of the assessment. Historically, the more decision oriented (for example, hiring oriented) an assessment's purpose, the more concise the report. The more development oriented an assessment's purpose, the more detailed the report. It may be useful to list the main set of report options from which to choose. All reports do not need to include all of these components. Some of these components may be in the decision-makers' report but not the development-oriented report that the assessed person sees:

a. Summary of purpose and methods. Often this section will also include competency definitions.

b. Summary of current scope and scale of responsibilities.

c. Summary of expertise in languages and countries in which he or she has resided for an extended, specified period of time.

d. Career summary in terms of position titles, organization names, and locations.

e. Concise executive summary of strengths and areas for development given the competencies and job specification involved in the situation.

f. Ratings of effectiveness regarding competencies and/or job specifications. The recommended scale for most senior executive situations is a five-point scale. As previously mentioned, specific indicators about what good looks like and what poor looks like for each competency and job specification are helpful to the process (for example, the BARS approach). They help introduce reliability into the assessment.

g. Norming and benchmarking mentioned above.

h. Prose descriptions and evaluative content for each major competency area of job specification.

i. Selection or hiring recommendation regarding a near-term decision.

j. Succession or next role recommendation regarding longer-term succession management.

k. Readiness/potential description and/or rating (sometimes in combination with current performance rating).

l. Initial recommendations regarding development actions. This may include not only weaknesses to fix, but the use of strengths in a new way. These actions are best finalized during a subsequent facilitated session between the person assessed and his or her manager (and perhaps the assessment provider and a representative from Human Resources) as described earlier.

m. Degree and timing of interest in relocating domestically and internationally.

n. Risk of voluntary departure and difficulty in replacing departed talent. I have found this type of risk management content to be very interesting and useful to CEOs and boards who want to know to what extent they need to be concerned about the retention of key senior executive talent.

5. Format of the Typical Senior Executive Assessment Report

It is my judgment that the senior executive assessment report (especially the report that is provided to the person being assessed) should be no more than 50% graphic in format (meaning ratings, tables, and graphs). The rest should be narrative or prose in format. Having a larger proportion of graphics can require a solitary reader to conduct too much interpretation on their own. Having a larger proportion of graphics also may indicate that too much of the report is being generated by a computer and not the analysis of an experienced and professional human being. While senior executive assessment should be rigorous, it should not be antiseptic or sparse. It should be nuanced and rich. Every word should be chosen purposefully for that particular report. CEO and board decision-makers, as well as senior executives who have been assessed, will all read these reports with a very critical eye. Precision is conveyed through customized word choice and thoughtful writing.

I have seen senior executive assessment report formats about individuals that are five pages long and others that are fifty pages long. The determining factors of length should be purpose of the assessment and the organization's/decision-makers' interest in detail. Development-oriented reports in a culture that stresses detail and thoroughness will be on the long end of the continuum. From my experience, the average length is around ten pages.

Regarding writing content, assessment writers differ in terms of whether most of the report contains summary content versus underlying rationale for the summary content. Some writers indicate specific examples from the assessment methodology (interviews and simulations, for example) that act as evidence for an overall observation. Often this can be convincing and compelling but it can add to the length of the report. Different organizations and purposes tend to influence report length. Detail-oriented and conservative organizations want more length. An emphasis on development often leads to more length as well. The other aspect of content that can vary is whether the content is primarily description versus prediction oriented. Again, this is based on the purpose of the assessment. Hiring assessment is primarily description of current behavioral tendencies and most succession-related assessment involves predictions and projections.

Two samples of concise assessment reports about individual senior executives are given in Figures 5.3 and 5.4. There are many types of report format that are longer and include more prose. The second report differs from the first in several ways: (1) the second report features purpose and methodology, (2) the second report indicates the languages spoken by the person assessed, (3) the second report was the result of a methodology that included cognitive testing – therefore a cognitive ability summary is in the report, (4) the competencies and competency ratings are broken up into several categories, (5) most of the writing is in bullet point format (we have found this format to be desired by many technology clients), (6) the assessment summary is at the end as opposed to the beginning, and (7) the second report includes less development detail (largely because the client was focused on a hiring decision; the first report was a succession and development report).

Stan Garrett

President, Consumer Solutions Group – Americas
XYZ Company

Written by: Jane Murphy
Kevin Davis

Personal and Confidential

Figure 5.3 Assessment report 1

Stan Garrett, President, Consumer Solutions Group – Americas, XYZ Company

Education:

MBA, University of Georgia, 1989
BS, Accounting, University of Southern Mississippi,1985

Career Experience:

From:	*To:*	*Position:*	*Company:*	*Location:*
2007	Present	President, Consumer Solutions Group, Americas	XYZ Company	New York, NY
2005	2007	Vice President, Strategy and Business Analysis	XYZ Company	New York, NY
2004	2005	Vice President, Planning	XYZ Company	Atlanta, GA
2000	2004	Vice President and General Manager, North America, Packaging Systems Division	XYZ Company	Atlanta, GA
1998	2000	Vice President, Strategy, South Division	XYZ Company	Atlanta, GA
1997	1998	Vice President, Asia Pacific and Latin America, Systems Division	XYZ Company	Atlanta, GA
1995	1996	Vice President, Operations, Systems Division	XYZ Company	Atlanta, GA

Stan Garrett, President, Consumer Solutions Group – Americas, XYZ Company

Career Experience:

From:	*To:*	*Position:*	*Company:*	*Location:*
1994	1995	Director, Corporate Planning	XYZ Company	Cleveland, OH
1992	1994	Director, Business Management	XYZ Company	Cleveland, OH
1990	1992	Director, Finance and Accounting	XYZ Company	Cleveland, OH
1986	1990	Financial Analyst	XYZ Company	Cleveland, OH

Figure 5.3 *Continued*

Stan Garrett, President, Consumer Solutions Group – Americas, XYZ Company

	Significant Developmental	Developmental	Performance	High Performance	Mastery
Integrity				▓	
Stewardship					▓
Business Acumen					▓
Organization Development				▓	
Teamwork/Collaboration			▓		
Global Perspective			▓		
Innovation				▓	
Commitment to Excellence				▓	

<u>OVERALL AREAS FOR DEVELOPMENT</u>

- His drive may cause him to want to be on the "right side" of every issue; he may move his point of view or opinion too frequently.
- He may use or depend on a core set of colleagues and miss opportunities to broaden his collaboration within his area of responsibility.
- His strategic nature may sometimes lead his communication style to be general; this can limit the impact of his coaching and his confronting of poor performance.
- He may also miss opportunities to clearly delegate to others around him.
- Still gaining experience globally.

<u>PRIMARY STRENGTHS</u>

- He will sort through complex and fast-moving situations.
- Highly versatile and adaptive.
- Strong emphasis on efficiency.
- Truly possesses a corporate-wide perspective.
- Things strategically about how to best position a given business.
- Possesses strong financial and marketing acumen.
- Connects well with customers.
- Personable and approachable in his style.
- Actively supports his team; open in giving credit and recognition.
- Combines having a reflective but active decision-making style.
- Possesses excellent presentation skills.
- Capable of charisma and persuasiveness.
- Able to be comfortable in a matrix structure.
- Interested in "thinking outside the box."
- He sees opportunity and takes initiative.

Stan Garrett, President, Consumer Solutions Group – Americas, XYZ Company

Integrity

1	2	3	4	5
Significant Developmental	Developmental	Performance	High Performance	Mastery

He is highly versatile. He is able to see situations in a multifaceted way. He sorts through complex and fast-moving situations effectively. Therefore, when problems occur, he is capable of adjusting to them and seeing a way forward. Others may at times see him as "spinning" or "positioning" while others may see him as an optimistic facilitator of action. He wants to have broad, widespread impact on the business to the point where one reference stated "he can end up flying at too high of a level."

Stewardship

1	2	3	4	5
Significant Developmental	Developmental	Performance	High Performance	Mastery

He thinks in terms of efficiency. He has acted in roles where he has had to lead downsizing and restructuring. He is thoughtful about organizational structure issues. He looks not just at cost but also examines the effectiveness of a business. He attends to human resources and capital resources in a combined and integrated way. He will raise the concept of sustainability with others. He has sought to audit and verify cost savings recently. Broadly speaking, he takes a corporate-wide perspective.

Figure 5.3 *Continued*

Stan Garrett, President, Consumer Solutions Group – Americas, XYZ Company

Business Acumen

1	2	3	4	5
Significant Developmental	Developmental	Performance	High Performance	Mastery

He appears to be an effective strategic thinker who conceives of how to best position a business. His overall financial and marketing acumen appear good. He most likely will do well with customers. He considers business drivers, decision-related tradeoffs, and broad implications regarding customers and suppliers when he makes decisions.

Organization Development

1	2	3	4	5
Significant Developmental	Developmental	Performance	High Performance	Mastery

He is personable and approachable. He is capable of building relationships with direct reports such that they feel loyalty toward him. People follow him. There are some who have said that he may sometimes use or depend on a core set of colleagues and miss opportunities to broaden his collaboration with his team. He does well in energizing groups and exciting people about the future of the business. His direction can be at a high or broad level. He often asks "where can I help and where can I get out of the way?" This general communication style may sometimes limit the impact of his coaching and confronting of poor performance. Nonetheless, he looks after, and is supportive of members of his team. He will often give credit and recognition to members of his team. He may be so busy at times that he misses opportunities to spend time with his direct reports. He may also miss opportunities to clearly delegate to others around him on occasion. He periodically will think through the competencies needed by his team in the future as he builds out his team. He, however, admits that he needs to continue to work on the definition of roles around him.

Stan Garrett, President, Consumer Solutions Group – Americas, XYZ Company

Teamwork/Collaboration

1	2	3	4	5
Significant Developmental	Developmental	Performance	High Performance	Mastery

He facilitates teams across a broad variety of areas. He possesses unique skills in influencing peers, including when he finds himself in a complex, matrix-oriented set of organizational dynamics. He is capable of charisma and persuasion. He possesses excellent presentation skills. He is often reflective and is rarely judgmental. He provokes thought more than giving others easy answers. This flexibility and thought, combined with his ambition, may cause him to be on the "right side of every issue." He can move his point of view based on what he sees as the needs of a situation or when he has learned something new. Subsequently, others around him may be confused as to what his opinion is about some issues. He needs to ensure he is as clear as possible when at the stage of giving direction.

Global Perspective

1	2	3	4	5
Significant Developmental	Developmental	Performance	High Performance	Mastery

He is different from many executives at XYZ Company in that he does not just know global markets, but also how the internal organization relates to each market. This being said, he is still learning in terms of his global business acumen although he reads new international situations well and is obtaining a fair amount of experience in South America.

Figure 5.3 *Continued*

Stan Garrett, President, Consumer Solutions Group – Americas, XYZ Company

Innovation

1	2	3	4	5
Significant Developmental	Developmental	Performance	High Performance	Mastery

He is interested in "pushing the envelope." He is not traditional in his thinking and wants to lead groups to think outside the box and be on the leading edge. He is an effective communicator who creates and articulates a vision about the future. He does not see limits, walls, or barriers that others see. He easily sees opportunity and wants to take initiative.

Commitment to Excellence

1	2	3	4	5
Significant Developmental	Developmental	Performance	High Performance	Mastery

He is dynamic and possesses a high level of energy. He appears to have taken packaging systems operations to the next level, developed the strategy function, and contributed to acquisitions. Leading the cost management initiative appears to have been a very difficult job as well. He is resourceful and flexible but persistent. He has a palpable edge to him but he is not over the top in his overt aggressiveness.

Stan Garrett, President, Consumer Solutions Group – Americas, XYZ Company

Suggested Areas for Development

1. He will find it beneficial to eliminate the potential for others to see him as "spinning" an issue and changing his opinion too frequently. Without some attention in this area there are others around him who may question whether they can trust him. As he knows, trust is a cornerstone for success now but also as he continues to gain more organizational responsibility.

2. We suggest he improve his systematic management processes, role definition, delegation and proactive coaching in his area of responsibility. While he is often very busy and he has been called on frequently to consult in an active manner with senior management, these aspects of people management within his area of responsibility deserve more of his attention. He will find that by investing his time in these areas it will allow him to play to the other strategic areas that interest him across time.

3. We encourage him to build out his international experience so that he can bolster his global business perspective. This will help him continue to broaden his view to an even greater extent. This will be useful as he continues to look at more senior management positions.

Figure 5.3 *Continued*

Purpose & Methodology

Purpose

- The purpose of this report is to provide executive assessment and development recommendations to be used for both individual leadership development and succession planning purposes.

Methodology

- Executives are assessed on both their background and experience and their leadership competencies. Background and experience are benchmarked against executives in similar roles in the market. Leadership competencies are benchmarked against an absolute scale for executive leadership.

- This report has been developed based on findings from:
    - Psychometric behavioral questionnaires (self-assessments) to understand styles and behaviors: OPQ, 16PF, HDS
    - Cognitive ability testing
    - In-depth interview with an industry and functional expert around knowledge and experience and a behavioural assessment specialist around leadership styles

---

Dan Moore – CV Summary

Career Experience

2007 – Present	President, Industry & Specialized Solutions Division (ISSD)	Sample Company	Atlanta, GA
2000 – 2007	President, Small Business Division (SBD)	Sample Company	Atlanta, GA
1998 – 2000	SVP and COO	Sample Company	Atlanta, GA
1997 – 1998	Vice President, General Manager New Products Strategic Business Unit	Sample Company	Atlanta, GA
1996 – 1997	Vice President, Product Manager	Sample Company	Atlanta, GA
1995 – 1996	Director, Product Management	Sample Company	Atlanta, GA
1991 – 1994	Product Line Manager	Sample Company	Atlanta, GA
1990 – 1991	Product Manager	Sample Company	Atlanta, GA

Other

Foreign languages: None

Qualifications

MSc in Management, Massachusetts Institute of Technology, USA

BSc in Electrical Engineering, University of Florida, USA

Figure 5.4 Assessment report 2

Dan Moore – Cognitive Ability Scores

Test	Description	Percentile	Accuracy
Verbal Reasoning	The ability to evaluate the logic of complex verbal information under pressure of time. Skills involved include drawing accurate inferences, identifying assumptions, making logical deductions and distinguishing between strong and weak arguments.	Average	65%
Numerical Reasoning	The ability to evaluate and draw accurate inferences from complex statistical data under pressure of time. Clearly an important skill in its own right, this is also an important intellectual underpinning of high-level strategic planning.	High	94%
Abstract Reasoning	The ability to think laterally and conceptually, to reason divergently with mental flexibility and deductive insight – important underpinnings of strategic ability and creative endeavor.	Average	65%

Overall

Dan's highest area of cognitive ability is numerical, where he is very effective in understanding and making use of complex financial data. His verbal and abstract reasoning skills are average, indicating that he will be similar to other managers in his use of verbal information and lateral thinking.

3

Dan Moore – Background & Experience	Rating Scale				
	1 Significant Development Area	**2** Development Area	**3** Sufficient	**4** Good	**5** Excellent

Competencies	Comment	Score
Scope of Responsibility	• Has run successively larger businesses with full operational control up to $180m • Has worked as part of "double-act" with Ray Vaughn for 13 years, focusing on operations vs. strategy	4
Technical/ Functional Knowledge	• Core financial, commercial expertise; very strong on business results • Good customer understanding which drives his activities	4.5
Industry Knowledge	• Excellent industry knowledge; insightful about competitors and differentiators, well networked • Able to communicate complex areas succinctly, e.g., "Quickbooks is easy, Sample Company is serious about business"	5
Business Acumen	• Makes decisions with clear analysis • Identified the key success factors of Sample Company business quickly and mobilized around them (e.g., customer service) • Has been very successful at implementation	4
Global Experience	• Saw the opportunity in global CRM and used it to good effect • Would consider move abroad for right opportunity, e.g., UK "if North America business improves"	4
Track Record	• Very impressive, yet understated, track record in life and career • Very modest about achievements and accomplishments, although they are substantial • Unusually long track record of success in Sample Company, especially considering ownership changes • Has been a lead executive for $18m revenue to $180m revenue over 16 years	4.5
	Average	4.3

4

Figure 5.4 *Continued*

Dan Moore – Leadership Competencies	Rating Scale				
	1 Significant Development Area	**2** Development Area	**3** Sufficient	**4** Good	**5** Excellent

Competencies	Comment	Score
Setting Strategy	• The strategy he develops is often in the form of plans that include metrics • Attempts to focus on core needs and opportunities for the business • Understands the multifaceted components of a given business model • Is vigilant and watchful about competitors in the market • However, many of the changes that he has driven through have come from elsewhere • Admitted that he can be slightly conservative or risk averse	3.5
Executing for Results	• Able to turn high-level goals into short-term plans (e.g., Power of One) • He is steady, reliable and persistent • Delivery, follow-through and progress on plans are important to him • Is highly focused on objectives • Seeks to define success-related metrics so he can confirm when he is successful in his endeavors	4.5
Leading Teams	• Defines "trusting relationships" as the core to leading teams • Shares responsibility with his team, "their problem is my problem," defends their interests • Seeks to match the right person to tasks and responsibilities • Takes performance reviews seriously and will give direct performance feedback periodically • Described by others as "competent, capable executive" rather than inspirational • While he will bring structure to a group's efforts, he may miss opportunities to motivate his team, by genuinely impacting emotions and motivations	3

5

Dan Moore – Leadership Competencies	Rating Scale				
	1 Significant Development Area	**2** Development Area	**3** Sufficient	**4** Good	**5** Excellent

Competencies	Comment	Score
Building Relationships & Using Influence	• Maintaining credibility, respect and a positive reputation are important to him • Respected for knowledge and uses this to build relationships (e.g., CEO) • Seeks to influence by proving his point of view; debates the merits of different options • Very strong content of message is lost by a flat communication style • Can possess low tolerance for people and processes that do not have a direct connection to results	3
Learning & Thinking	• Practical problem solver who is analytical and logical; evaluates information; challenges others • Learns lessons from his own experience and doesn't repeat them (e.g., Roll-out of new product) • Changes his views and actions in face of new information (e.g., Sample Company focus on customers/support) • Takes a disciplined approach to identify strengths and weaknesses in the business	4
Interpersonal Acumen	• Has a straightforward, direct and utilitarian manner • Others may see him as closed or guarded on occasion • While he is often reserved, he also wants to be recognized and noticed by others • Observes others and appears to understand them accurately • Would benefit from ensuring he has a critical mass of facts before challenging and doubting others	3
Motivations	• Motivated by the value brought to customers, "I love what we do" • Wants to see the company success; has a real will and responds well when in underdog position • Competitive and wants to be distinctively and substantively successful • Wants to be seen as competent and valuable • Thrives on activity and is involved in a variety of issues	3.5
	Average	**3.5**

6

Figure 5.4 *Continued*

Dan Moore – Summary

Key Strengths	Key Areas for Development
• Long-term track record in managing and growing business • Very knowledgeable about competitors and networked in the market • Steady, reliable, and persistent in meeting objectives • Focused on follow-through and delivery • Analytical and logical approach; strong with numbers	• Developing a more impactful communication style, which will help in motivating his team and building relationships • Being more open to new approaches and appropriate risk • Ensuring he has all the facts of a situation before challenging and doubting others

Summary

Dan is a highly experienced and successful manager of a large-scale business. He uses data and analysis to develop plans and is competitive and determined in driving outcomes. He has been working in partnership with Ray for many years and is now in the process of growing beyond his operations-oriented and somewhat utilitarian approach. He can leverage his keen competitive insights to take calculated risks more frequently, actively experimenting with others' ideas. He would also benefit from communications training to adapt and develop his influencing styles, more overtly celebrating successes and energizing others.

7

Figure 5.4 *Continued*

6. Legal Issues and Information Management

Senior executive assessment needs to be relevant to a given organization situation and job. This is why the competency and job specification process is so important. Informed individuals (CEOs, board members) need to be thoroughly interviewed so that a proper analysis of the needs of the situation can take place. This helps prevent the use of impertinent questions in an interview.

Different senior executive assessment providers have different points of view about how broad, personal, and open-ended a senior-level assessment process should be. The rationale for some is that a senior executive brings their total self to their job – their entire personality, character, and 24-hour day. Therefore, much is fair game. For example, a segment of senior executive assessment providers interview family members. CEOs and boards need to decide what their comfort level is regarding the personal nature of an assessment process.

Methods, tools, and reporting should not lead to adverse impact with regard to minority groups. The particular challenge here is that it has been my experience that some cognitive measures may not accurately depict cognitive functioning in minority groups. For this reason, great care must be taken when making use of this type of measure and when setting "cutoff" scores overall across different types of measures. In general, I am not a fan of setting cutoff scores in senior executive assessment given that senior executive performance is multidimensional and complex. I believe that there are many ways to obtain senior executive success overall.

Data privacy and control of information are also important topics. Senior executive assessments often contain information that those assessed would consider sensitive. Therefore, the assessment provider needs to receive consent to proceed, not only after describing the overall process but specifically after describing who will be debriefed about the assessment, who will see the reports, as well as how reports and data will be used and stored. With the explosion of the Internet and electronic databases, data privacy has become an even more important topic. Data privacy laws in Europe recently have become more stringent, for example. I strongly advocate the inclusion of policy about how the information will be used and not used within main project communications, subsequent policy documents, and in the assessment reports themselves.

7. International Assessment

Speaking of Europe, the promised globalization of the capital markets and business overall truly has arrived over the past decade or so. Therefore, organizations and their senior executive talent have become more international in nature. A given executive team is more likely to consist of people from different cultures and countries than ever before.

Indeed, the competency of being able to adjust to executive assignments outside of one's native country appears on many senior executive competency lists these days. Specific assessment tools designed to measure this area soon will be in demand. Eric Noel and his colleagues at ACT are in the midst of validating and finalizing a self-report questionnaire that can help predict senior executive expatriate success.

The other question is how to assess talent located around the globe in a way that is standardized but also takes into account the uniqueness of the local culture. One way is to develop and use country- and region-specific norms and benchmarking when interpreting self-report questionnaires and other methods. Sometimes this comparison data is difficult to obtain. Another way is to develop tools (such as self-report leadership questionnaires) that include content, wording, and questions that can be applied around the world, across countries and cultures. A third way is to structure assessment work so that there is a core set of competencies and job specifications, yet people familiar with local cultures can take part in local interviews, conduct local multi-source interviewing, and partner in the interpretation of personality/leadership style measures and in the writing of reports. In this way, the most effective comparisons can be made, for example, when comparing a CEO's direct reports who are located around the world.

8. Assessment as an Organizational Change Tool

The process of assessment in itself can lead to organizational/culture change. This is because the assessment process is in part a communications tool. It shows the people who are assessed what the CEO and board members consider important. If the competencies of Collaboration and Global Acumen are featured prominently in an assessment process, individuals who are exposed to the assessment process (those assessed as well as multi-source reference providers) will attend to ways to be more collaborative and global in their activities. They now know that these items are at top of mind when their boss is evaluating them.

Another way assessment can change organizational cultures is by creating a higher standard for openness and disclosure in senior executive teams. Assessment opens people up. It lowers walls and causes people to ask more questions of themselves and of others. It sets a tone of "I am not perfect" and "this is what I am working on." Many CEOs have reported to me that the result of their team going through an assessment is that senior executives are more apt to put their true thinking "on the table," for example in executive committee meetings. This leads to more transparent and effective deliberations about major decisions. It prevents "groupthink."

9. Decision-Making Based on Assessment

Senior executives and potential senior executives are complicated people. At the end of an assessment process, a CEO and board are still frequently faced with a complex set of tradeoffs amongst candidates. There are two items that are important when addressing assessment-related decision-making. First, organizations should not position assessment itself as the main decision-making method. The truth is that assessment is one of a handful of inputs about a senior executive. Positioning assessment as the decision-maker causes the real decision-makers not to "own" a given decision. This positioning will also put undue pressure on the candidate who is experiencing the assessment.

Second, given the complexity, senior executive assessment-related decisions rarely are easy. Here are the practical approaches I have found to be most useful in yielding effective selection or placement decisions:

a. Do not forget to review the competencies and job specification. Sometimes decision-makers with the best of intentions start with competencies and specifications, but they do not finish with them. If necessary, clarify or analyze again what are the priorities. Do not undervalue or ignore "failure factors."
b. Create an open debate amongst decision-makers and those in senior positions who will have to live with the decision.
c. Visualize the candidate in the role interacting with key people or groups (for example, presenting in front of the board).
d. Identify actual people who represent what you want or do not want in the position. Compare and contrast candidates to these positive and negative models.
e. Do not undervalue or ignore negative multi-source interview insights and information.

10. Measuring the Effectiveness of Senior Executive Assessment

Some assessment providers (internal or external) administer a survey and conduct phone calls with each of their clients after a given project is completed. As an example, my clients are asked to rate and describe five dimensions of a senior executive assessment project: (1) accuracy of insights and usefulness of recommendations; (2) quality of project management; (3) urgency of response; (4) quality of communication; and (5) value of the project given the fee/price of the services. Annually, each of the scales averages close to a 4.5 on a five-point scale.

This approach, however, does not lead to a clear understanding of the assessment's impact on business and organizational results. Rob Kaiser, Robert Hogan, and Bart Craig recently[1] stated that it was frequently the case that leadership research, including senior leadership research, examined leadership's influence on others' approval and rarely examined senior leadership's influence on broader organization levels of business performance. Two studies that are exceptions are noted in the first chapter of this book.

How useful is assessment in discerning and predicting which executives will be a success and which ones will not? Nothing substitutes for examining the association between competency ratings or assessment report recommendations and how an assessed person's performance plays out. I highly recommend that the association between the assessment and effectiveness be analyzed periodically in a given organization and with a given methodology so that effectiveness in that context can be understood. The other benefit of this type of study is that improvements to the assessment methods can be made.

The article by Kaiser, Hogan, and Craig provides four areas of direction regarding these types of business-oriented studies. First, no organization level of performance is perfect. There is no one best way to measure the success of a company. Multiple effective criteria are better than one. Second, it is better to look at multiple stock prices for the same company before the senior executive assessment project and then after the project is completed. Otherwise, something unique to a company's situation and industry could be driving the stock up. Third, the type of business results chosen for the study should relate to the level of the people being assessed. It can be argued as to whether overall stock price is just the domain of the CEO or whether senior executives other than CEOs have enough influence on stock price. My opinion is that stock price is a good results indicator for senior executives. Fourth, on a related point, the researchers suggest that approximately two to three years need to elapse to allow for an evaluation of senior executive actions.

11. Tips: How to Get the Most out of Internal and External Senior Executive Assessment

The Tips box on the next page lists practical suggestions about how to make the best use of senior executive assessment consulting resources, both internally and externally.

The Future of Senior Executive Assessment

In closing, below are some of my predictions about future trends in senior executive assessment. These are nothing more than educated guesses. For example, the impact of technology has been difficult to predict. Advances that I would have expected based on improvements to data and video technology have not proceeded as fast as I would have expected to date. Perhaps this is due to the persistent notion held by many CEOs and board members that the assessment of senior executives should not be mechanical or occur remotely. At the least, I hope these thoughts prompt brainstorming and new thinking in senior executive assessment:

a. As we see drastic changes in globalization of business activities, markets, and organizations, assessment practices must adapt in alignment with these shifts. As I previously mentioned within the international assessment section, the globalization of today's businesses has led to changes in the competencies necessary for success as well as the tools and methodologies used in the assessment process. Global agility is becoming a more frequently included competency within senior executive assessment work.

b. Lists of competencies can be too long. The result can be a disparate laundry list of desirable attributes. In addition, members of the board of a $7 billion chemicals company were clear with me that "integrative" content is important when directing what is to be measured and emphasized in senior executive assessment, not just a bland and disconnected list.

Tips:
How to Get the Most out of Internal and External Senior Executive Assessment Professionals

1. Use a group that genuinely specializes in senior-level executive assessment.
2. Ask how long the senior executive assessment group has been in existence. Ask about the experience level of the assessment professionals in the group.
3. Engage actively in the discussion about the purpose of the assessment with the assessment professionals. Ask for relevant examples of work.
4. Read a sample report to make sure it is not too general or reads like a "horoscope."
5. Ensure that interviewers and those who conduct multi-source interviews possess personalities such that they can develop rapport with interviewees and those who provide referencing information.
6. Create competencies and/or job specifications/requirements that are not too lengthy, are very specific, and are relevant to that organization's situation.
7. Ensure that external assessment professionals do not force their set of competencies onto you. While they should bring a point of view and seek to understand preexisting competencies, the main objective is for the competencies to be as organization and job specific as possible.
8. Ensure report formats are customized to your needs and preferences as much as is practical.
9. Clarify how and when the assessed individuals will receive assessment feedback before the project starts. Clarify data privacy and report distribution.
10. Schedule the delivery of the verbal presentation and the delivery of reports to decision-makers before the project starts.
11. In larger group projects, consider having the senior-most executive assessed. If this is part of the plan, have the senior-most executive assessed first. It models effective collaboration, gives the project useful momentum, and this first assessment can be used to make any initial adjustments to the process.
12. Develop and implement a clear communications plan so that all of those involved understand the assessment.
13. Ensure balance between methodologies, for example, the use of interviews and self-report questionnaires.
14. When working with an external firm, favor the use of full-time employees on the consulting team whenever practical so that quality can be assured.
15. Ensure that senior executive assessment reports are not written primarily by a computer and the mechanical derivation of assessment report prose.
16. Ask many questions as you receive and actively digest assessment information and reports.
17. Clarify ahead of time how and when the assessed individuals will work with others to finalize an effective development plan.
18. Ensure that senior management follows up periodically via a schedule and specifically about development objectives and plans.

c. The properties of video technology will change the way assessment interviews and other meetings are conducted. Assessment professionals and those assessed appear to be more accepting of video meetings. Gone are the staccato images and audio that disrupt the rhythm of conversations and interviews.

d. Video already has changed the nature of deliverables in assessment on occasion. For example, as opposed to the interview just being a means to a written assessment report, the National Football League records my interviews with high-potential coaches and front office managers via video. The League makes DVD copies available to all teams in the League upon request, so that high-potential talent can be exposed across more parts of the organization/geographies and so that the sharing of talent/risk-taking in selection in the overall organization can be increased. I also provide feedback based on my review of the DVD (the interviewee also receives and views the same copy).

This program has had several positive outcomes: (1) Diversity in the Head Coach position has grown from 2 of the 32 teams to 6 of the 32 teams during this program (5 of the 6 Head Coaches who fit into diversity categories have gone through this program). (2) More first-time Head Coaches are being selected. (3) Owners and other decision-makers use these DVDs to finalize their in-person interview invitees. (4) Owners and other decision-makers use these DVDs to prepare for their in-person interviews. (5) Communications managers for the teams attempt to predict a candidate's effectiveness with the press through these DVDs. (6) The DVDs are used to "double check" a candidate during final deliberations after the in-person interview. In a similar way, Talent Management executives at SAP have asked me if a regular video conference interview could be recorded so that the interview (or parts of it) could be reviewed by decision-makers.

e. Improvements in technology should continue to hasten the electronic delivery of simulations and work samples.

f. Becoming more specific about subtypes of experience/track record and their ability to predict success in certain situations will continue. Remember the Gerstner/IBM example. This mapping is inexact at present. Also, from a development perspective, what is the optimal ordering of development experiences? Novartis has labeled these major development experience categories as:

changing divisions, turnarounds, strategic demands, influencing without authority, international assignments, moving from line to staff, projects/task forces, size, complexity, people demands, and start-ups. If the objective is building a great senior-level general manager, what experiences (and what order) are most important? Some researchers and consultants consider this area to be more important than personality and behavioral style. Better measurement and validation in this area are needed.

g. While some people see the term "senior executive teamwork" as oxymoronic and are skeptical of the notion that it could or should truly exist because of internal competition, those who believe in its value would be better served if organizational researchers developed a more specific understanding of the personal and contextual factors involved in making it happen.

h. Potential senior executives may need to be identified earlier due to the shortage of talent/war for talent so that development specialists can have the gift of time in helping to realize these individuals' potential. These organizations can also more overtly make attempts to retain these individuals.

i. Multi-source interviews over the phone, in person, and via video may become more frequently used than 360 degree surveys due to the richness and nuance in the information received.

Summary

The increasing complexity and dynamic nature of the world is changing what we need and expect from the people who run our largest organizations. Yet I have always been surprised by how disorganized and incomplete CEOs and boards have been in evaluating their most important resource – the people around them. This last chapter, and this whole book, attempts to "arm" the reader with a systematic and useful understanding of the professional options available in making these important decisions.

My hope is that the increased use of senior executive assessment might have a supplementary positive impact on the world's organizations. Throughout much of this book, I have mentioned how senior executive assessment should be centered around the needs of an organization so that the right people can be identified to make that organization succeed. Because the use of senior executive assessment involves this in-depth thinking about the strengths and weaknesses of an organization, and should involve a real attempt to understand where an organization is headed, the process of executive assessment in itself may lead to more critical thinking about the risks and threats associated with an organization's strategy and tactics. In essence, people vigilance can lead back to strategic vigilance. In this way, we may be spared catastrophic economic crises in the future and be more assured of growth.

Notes

Notes

Chapter 1

1 Weiner & Mahoney (1981)
2 Joyce, Nohria, & Roberson (2003)
3 Sorcher (1985)
4 Smart (1999)
5 Harding & Rouse (2007)
6 Smart (1998)
7 Byham, Smith, & Paese (2002)
8 Bossidy & Charan (2002)
9 Charan (2005)

Chapter 2

1 Church (2006)
2 Conger & Fulmer (2003)

Chapter 3

1 Dotlich & Cairo (2003)
2 Finkelstein (2003)
3 Lencioni (2002)
4 Layden (2008)
5 Eichinger, Lombardo, & Raymond (2004)
6 Menkes (2006)
7 Goleman, Boyatzis, & McKee (2002)

8 Sessa & Taylor (2000)
9 Khurana (2002)
10 Michaels, Handfield-Jones, & Axelrod (2001)
11 Charan, Drotter, & Noel (2001)
12 Gerstner (2003)
13 Reingold (2008)
14 Frisch (1998)
15 Marcus, Blank, & Andelman (1999)

Chapter 4

1 Frisch (1998)

Chapter 5

1 Kaiser, Hogan, & Craig (2008)

References

Anders, G. (2006, January 16). When filling top jobs makes sense – and when it doesn't. *Wall Street Journal*, p. B1.

Bossidy, L., & Charan, R. (2002). *Execution: The discipline of getting things done*. New York: Crown Business.

Byham, W. C., Smith, A. B., & Paese, M. J. (2002). *Grow your own leaders: How to identify, develop, and retain leadership talent*. Upper Saddle River, NJ: Prentice Hall.

Charan, R. (2005). Ending the CEO succession crisis. *Harvard Business Review, 83* (2), 72–81.

Charan, R., Drotter, S., & Noel, J. (2001). *The leadership pipeline: How to build the leadership-powered company*. San Francisco: Jossey-Bass.

Church, A. (May, 2006). *Talent management: Will the high potentials please stand up?* Paper presented at the 21st annual meeting of the Society for Industrial-Organizational Psychology, Dallas, TX.

Conger, J. A., & Fulmer, R. M. (2003). Developing your leadership pipeline. *Harvard Business Review, 81* (12), 76–84.

Dotlich, D. L., & Cairo, P. C. (2003). *Why CEOs fail: The 11 behaviors that can derail your climb to the top – and how to manage them*. San Francisco: Jossey-Bass.

Eichinger, R. W., Lombardo, M. M., & Raymond, C. C. (2004). *FYI for talent management: The talent management handbook*. Minneapolis: Lominger Limited.

Finkelstein, S. (2003). *Why smart executives fail and what you can learn from their mistakes*. New York: Portfolio.

Frisch, M. H. (1998). Designing the individual assessment process. In R. Jeanneret & R. Silzer (Eds.), *Individual psychological assessment:*

Predicting behavior in organizational settings (pp. 135–177). San Francisco: Jossey-Bass.

Gerstner, L. V. (2003). *Who says elephants can't dance?* New York: Harper Collins.

Goleman, D., Boyatzis, R., & McKee, A. (2002). *Primal leadership: Learning to lead with emotional intelligence.* Boston: Harvard Business School Press.

Harding, D., & Rouse, T. (2007, October 2). Human due diligence. *Wall Street Journal*, p. A16.

Joyce, W. F., Nohria, N., & Roberson, B. (2003). *What really works.* New York: Harper Business.

Kaiser, R. B., Hogan, R., & Craig, S. B. (2008). Leadership and the fate of organizations. *American Psychologist, 63* (2), 96–110.

Khurana, R. (2002). *Searching for a corporate savior: The irrational quest for charismatic CEOs.* Princeton, NJ: Princeton University Press.

Layden, T. (2008). And one for all. *Sports Illustrated, 108* (3), 30–33.

Lencioni, P. (2002). *The five dysfunctions of a team: A leadership fable.* San Francisco: Jossey-Bass.

Marcus, B., Blank, A., & Andelman, B. (1999). *Built from scratch: How a couple of regular guys grew the Home Depot from nothing to $30 billion.* New York: Crown Business.

Menkes, J. (2006). *Executive intelligence: What all great leaders have.* New York: Harper Collins.

Michaels, E., Handfield-Jones, H., & Axelrod, B. (2001). *The war for talent.* Boston: Harvard Business School Press.

Reingold, J. (2008). Meet your new leader. *Fortune, 158* (10), 145–146.

Sessa, V. I., & Taylor, J. J. (2000). *Executive selection: Strategies for success.* San Francisco: Jossey-Bass.

Smart, B. D. (1999). *Topgrading: How leading companies win by hiring, coaching, and keeping the best people.* New York: Prentice Hall Press.

Smart, G. H. (1998). *Management assessment methods in venture capital: Towards a theory of human capital valuation.* Doctoral dissertation, Claremont Graduate University.

Sorcher, M. (1985). *Predicting executive success: What it takes to make it into senior management.* New York: John Wiley & Sons.

Weiner, N., & Mahoney, T. A. (1981). A model of corporate performance as a function of environmental, organizational, and leadership influences. *Academy of Management Journal, 24*, 453–470.

Names Index

Andelman, B.   142n15
Axelrod, B.   142n10

Blank, A.   62, 142n15
Bossidy, L.   10, 141n8
Boyatzis, R.   46, 141n7(ch 3)
Byham, W. C.   9, 141n7(ch 1)

Cairo, P. C.   40, 141n1(ch 3)
Charan, R.   12, 54, 141n9, 142n11
Church, A.   141n1(ch 2)
Conger, J. A.   32, 141n2(ch 2)
Craig, S. B.   134, 142n1

Dotlich, D. L.   40, 141n1(ch 3)
Drotter, S.   54, 142n11

Eichinger, R. W.   37, 44,
    141n5(ch 3)

Finkelstein, S.   40, 141n2(ch 3)
Frisch, M. H.   61, 102, 142n14,
    142n1
Fulmer, R. M.   32, 141n2(ch 2)

Gerstner, L. V.   56–7, 137, 142n12

Goleman, D.   45–6, 141n7(ch 3)

Handfield-Jones, H.   142n10
Hogan, R.   40, 93, 134, 142n1

Joyce, W. F.   8, 141n2(ch 1)

Kaiser, R. B.   134, 142n1
Khurana, R.   47, 142n9

Layden, T.   40, 141n4(ch 3)
Lencioni, P.   40, 141n3(ch 3)
Lombardo, M. M.   37, 44,
    141n5(ch 3)

Mahoney, T. A.   8, 141n1(ch 1)
Marcus, B.   62, 142n15
McKee, A.   46, 141n7(ch 3)
Menkes, J.   45, 141n6
Michaels, E.   54, 142n10

Noel, E.   131
Noel, J.   54, 142n11
Nohria, N.   8, 141n2(ch 1)

Paese, M. J.   141n7(ch 1)

Raymond, C. C.   141n5
Reingold, J.   58, 142n13
Roberson, B.   8, 141n2

Sessa, V. I.   46, 142n8
Smart, B. D.   141n4(ch 1)
Smart, G. H.   9, 141n6(ch 1)

Smith, A. B.   9, 141n7(ch 1)
Sorcher, M.   141n3(ch 1)

Taylor, J. J.   46, 142n8

Weiner, N.   8, 141n1(ch 1)

Subject Index

16PF   79
360 degree surveys   32, 68, 90–2, 97, 98, 104–5, 138

accuracy
    cornerstone of effective assessment   5
    rating scales (BARS)   76
    structured interviews   74
AlliedSignal   10
American Express   57
assessment, who should conduct   66–8
assessment factors   43
assessment material, retention of   102
assessment methods, what to use   96–7
assessment professionals
    clinical psychologists as 3–4
    different approaches   65, 85
    executive search firms   68
    focus on behavioral qualities   35, 70
    getting most out of   136

human resources-oriented firms   67–8
    multi-year consulting arrangements   26
    networking   4
    psychology-oriented firms   67
assessment program, as retention tool   18

behavioral style   41
Behaviorally Anchored Rating Scales (BARS)   38, 75, 76, 120
benchmarking   117–18, 118(fig.)
    country- and region-specific   132
    executive search firms   68
board assessment, subset of   7
board members
    as clients   114–15
    in risk management business   12–13
    informed individuals   130
Built from Scratch   62
business models, changes in   31
business schools   3

California Personality
    Inventory 79
Cambria Consulting 73
candidate pool 3
case scenarios
    culture change 61
    external and internal candidate
        assessment 18
    private equity due diligence 29
    spin off 31
    succession management 25–6
Case Western Reserve Weatherhead
    School of Management 3
CEOs
    as clients 114–15
    executive team reviews 20
    informed individuals 130
    participation in assessment
        101
    selection of 12
CFO
    assessment report on 32, 114
    good communication 57–8
    identity of bosses 51
    risk and 24–5
charisma 46–7, 49, 50, 51
Citigroup 20
coaching 109–13
cognitive ability 84–8
communication
    with assessee 105
    with board 114–15
    CFO and 57–8
    clear plan 136
    with organization 107
    to participants 115
    project plan 98–9, 105, 136
competencies 35, 37–40, 62–3,
    70–1
    BARS 76
    of CFO 57–8
    'Hybrid' interviews 72–3

lists too long 135
confidentiality 91
Corporate Director's
    Guidebook 11–12
corporate governance 1, 10–14
Culture Analyst Culture Fit
    Index 82, 84(fig.)
culture surveys 59–60, 62, 81–4
cutoff scores 131

data privacy 131
debrief presentation 101
decision-making
    based on assessment 133
    cognitive judgment 85–6
    functions of board 7
    intuition in 1
    potential for 56
Denison's Organizational Culture
    Survey (DOCS) 81
derailers 35, 40, 80 *see also*
    failure factors
Development Decisions
    International 55
development plan/planning
    sessions 98–103, 103(fig.)
developmental assessments 32–3
DSM-IV 94
dual capability 42–4
due diligence
    human 8–9
    markets and business
        models 31
    mergers and acquisitions 8, 30
    private equity 15, 29
    venture capital 15, 27
DVDs 137

economic crisis 2008 57–8
ego, excessive 40–1, 47, 63
Egon Zehnder 68
emotional intelligence 45–6

ethics   58–9
*Execution: The Discipline of Getting
   Things Done*   10
executive coaches   27, 107
executive intelligence   45
exposure   22–6, 25(fig.)   *see also*
   risk

failure factors   40–1, 47, 63
   see also derailers
faking   79
family members, interviews
   with   130
feedback
   assessments as development   32
   external candidates   101–2
   negative from colleagues   91
   respectfulness and   30
   use of DVDs   137
fiduciary responsibility   11
fit   63
   integrity/ethics   58–9
   organizational culture   59–61
   potential   55–6
   scope and scale   54–5
   strategy/tactics   56–8

ghSmart   72
globalization   14, 131–2, 135

Hewitt Associates   68
hiring
   casual decisions   2
   importance of   1
   poor outcomes   6, 8
   purpose of assessment   16–17
hiring decisions, poor outcomes   6
Hogan Assessment Systems   80,
   93
Hogan Development Survey
   (HDS)   94, 95–6
Home Depot   62

human capital
   critical component   33–4
   valuation of   13
human resources function,
      assessments carried out by
   internal   67, 97
Human Synergistics' Organizational
   Culture Inventory (OCI)   81

IBM   56–7
*Individual Psychological
   Assessment*   61, 102
integrity   58–9, 92–6
internal talent   13–14, 17
international assessment   131–2,
   135
interpersonal skills   46
interviews   68–78, 104–5
   behavioral   70–2
   best practices   73–5
   chronological   72
   hybrid approaches   72–3
   para-clinical   69
   questions   71–2, 76–8
   situational   69–70
   structured versus
      unstructured   74
   video recording of   137, 138

Kaiser Permanente   37
Kaplan DeVries Inc.   44

'leadership recipe' books   36, 53
learning agility   44–5

markets, changes in   31, 131,
   135
McBer & Company   37
mergers and acquisitions   8–9,
   29–30
Merrill Lynch   20
minority groups   131

motivation 80
Motorola 97

narcissism 48–51, 94
  assessing narcissists 50–1
  narcissistic rage 49
  productive narcissist 49–50
National Football League 40, 137
negative personality factors *see*
    derailers
NEO PI-R 79
networking 4
New England Patriots 40–1
norms 115–17
  country- and
      region-specific 132

objectivity
  lack of in CEOs and boards 2
  rating scales 75
Occupational Personality
    Questionnaire-32
    (OPQ-32) 79
Oliver Wyman 68
onboarding 17
openness 83, 132
organizational change, assessment
    as tool for 132
organizational culture 59–61,
    81–4
  choosing assessment methods
      and 97

performance
  improvement 31
  and potential 22–3
  see also competencies; cognitive
      ability
personality 40–7
  disorders/weaknesses 47–51
  integrity tests 95–6
  motivation different to 80

self-report questionnaires 66,
    78–9, 86–7
Personnel Decisions
    International 55
planning, senior executive
    assessments 105 *see also*
    succession planning;
    development plan/planning
    sessions
potential, assessing 20, 22,
    23(fig.), 54–6
previous results 41, 51–2
*Primal Leadership: Learning to Lead
    with Emotional
    Intelligence* 46
private equity 8, 15, 27–9, 72
promotions 17
  cost of failures 8
psychologists 3–4, 6, 37, 41, 94

Raven's Progressive Matrices
    85
reports
  components 118–20
  length of 121
  samples 122–30 (figs.)
respectfulness 30
retention 9, 18, 138
risk
  assessment mitigates 12–13
  succession plans and 22–7
RHR International 67
RJR Nabisco 56
role plays 90
Russell Reynolds Associates 68,
    82

SAP 2, 137
Sarbanes–Oxley Act (SOX) 11
*Searching for a Corporate Savior:
    The Irrational Quest for
    Charismatic CEOs* 47

self-importance *see* narcissism
self-report questionnaires 66,
  78–9, 86–7
senior executive, definition of 7
Senior Executive Assessment
  Factors 42–7, 51, 53, 55, 62,
  78
senior executive team
  reviews 19–20
SHL Group Ltd. (SHL) 80
simulations and work samples 68,
  88–90
  case analysis and
    presentation 89
  electronic delivery of 137
  homework 88–9
  inbox exercise 89
  leaderless discussions 89–90
  role plays 90
spin off, case scenario 31
stock prices 8, 57, 134
sub-prime mortgage lending
  crisis 20
succession assessment
  different to promotion
    assessment 22
  employee fears 26–7
  what to assess 61
succession lists 21
succession management 9, 20–7
  connected to development
    33

exposure 22–6, 25(fig.)
  planning most important
    issue 12

talent management 16, 33–4
teams/teamwork
  assessing the CEO 101
  dynamics of 40–1
  reviews 19–20
  succession management 20–7
  VC and PE due dilligence 27–9
  viewed as oxymoronic 138
technology
  future use of 135, 137
  installation and testing 2
Towers Perrin 68
toxic leadership 47–51
TPG 37
turnarounds 31
TXU Energy 51

venture capital
  benefits of assessment 8–9, 27
  use of chronological
    interviews 72
video technology 135, 137

War for Talent 54
Watson Glaser Critical Thinking
  Appraisal 85
Workplace Technologies Research
  Inc. (WTRI) 86, 89